The Politics of Refugees in South Asia

Partition and post-colonial migrations—sometimes voluntary, often forced—have created borders in South Asia that serve to oppress rather than protect. Migrants and refugees feel that their real homes lie beyond the borders, and liberation struggles continue the quest for freedoms that have proved to be elusive for many. States scapegoat refugees as "outsiders" for their own ends, justifying the denial of their rights, while academic discourse on refugees represents them either as victims or as terrorists. Taking a stance against such projections, this book examines refugees' struggles for better living conditions and against marginalization.

By analyzing protest and militarization among refugees, the book argues that they are neither victims without agency nor war entrepreneurs. Through interviews, surveys, and statistical analyses, it shows how states have manipulated refugee identity and resistance to promote the ideal of the nation-state, thereby creating protracted refugee crises. This is evident even in the most humanitarian state intervention in modern South Asia—India's military intervention in East Pakistan (now Bangladesh) in 1971.

The findings put forward provide the basis for understanding the conditions under which violence can break out, and thereby have implications for host countries, donor countries, and aid organizations in the formulation of refugee policy. The book is of interest to scholars in the fields of South Asian studies, comparative politics, international relations, refugee studies, development studies, security studies, and peace studies.

Navine Murshid is Assistant Professor of Political Science at Colgate University, Hamilton, New York, USA. Her research interests include South Asian politics, international political economy, civil wars, economic development, and refugee and minority politics.

Routledge Advances in South Asian Studies

Edited by Subrata K. Mitra, South Asia Institute, University of Heidelberg, Germany

South Asia, with its burgeoning, ethnically diverse population, soaring economies, and nuclear weapons, is an increasingly important region in the global context. The series, which builds on this complex, dynamic and volatile area, features innovative and original research on the region as a whole or on the countries. Its scope extends to scholarly works drawing on history, politics, development studies, sociology and economics of individual countries from the region as well those that take an interdisciplinary and comparative approach to the area as a whole or to a comparison of two or more countries from this region. In terms of theory and method, rather than basing itself on any one orthodoxy, the series draws broadly on the insights germane to area studies, as well as the toolkit of the social sciences in general, emphasizing comparison, the analysis of the structure and processes, and the application of qualitative and quantitative methods. The series welcomes submissions from established authors in the field as well as from young authors who have recently completed their doctoral dissertations.

The Politics of Refugees in South Asia

Identity, resistance, manipulation

Navine Murshid

Routledge
Taylor & Francis Group

LONDON AND NEW YORK

First published 2014
by Routledge
2 Park Square, Milton Park, Abingdon, Oxfordshire OX14 4RN

and by Routledge
711 Third Avenue, New York, NY 10017

First issued in paperback 2015

Routledge is an imprint of the Taylor & Francis Group, an informa business

British Library Cataloguing in Publication Data
A catalogue record for this book is available from the British Library

Library of Congress Cataloging in Publication Data
Murshid, Navine.
  The politics of refugees in South Asia : identity, resistance, manipulation /
Navine Murshid.
    pages cm. – (Routledge advances in South Asian studies ; 24)
    Includes bibliographical references and index.
    1. Refugees–Political aspects–South Asia. 2. Forced migration–Political
aspects–South Asia. I. Title.
    HV640.4.S64M87 2013
    325'.210954–dc23
                        2013012183

ISBN 13: 978-1-138-94846-4 (pbk)
ISBN 13: 978-0-415-62930-0 (hbk)

Typeset in Times New Roman
by Taylor & Francis Books

Dedicated to my brother, Shabab Murshid
(January 13, 1990–May 10, 2005)

Contents

Illustrations

Acknowledgements

A vast network of people—mentors, colleagues, students, family, friends, and acquaintances—from North America to South Asia made this book possible and I thank you all.

First I thank my mentors Jim Johnson, Bing Powell, and Randy Stone at the University of Rochester for guiding and inspiring me to work on the subject of refugees, both during and after the dissertation stage of the research that went into this book.

I thank my colleagues and friends at the University of Rochester for their friendship and all kinds of discussions pertaining to the book and otherwise: Subhasish Ray, Kankana Mukhopadhyay, Arnd Plagge, Daniel Gillion, Fabiana Machado, and Martin Steinwand.

At Colgate University I have been fortunate to find many supportive colleagues. In particular, I would like to thank Ed Fogarty, Illan Nam, Dan Epstein, Noah Dauber, Fred Chernoff, Michael Johnston, Bruce Rutherford, Tim Byrnes, Eliza Kent, Noor Khan, Stanley Brubaker, Manny Teodoro, and last but not least our administrative assistant, Cynthia Terrier, who has made my life at Colgate University run smoothly. At Jawaharlal Nehru University I thank Jayati Ghosh, Anuradha Chenoy, and Sanjay Bhardwaj for making my stay in New Delhi productive and comfortable. I also thank Nagesh Rao, Pothik Ghosh, Paramita Ghosh, Prasanta Chakravarty, Saroj Giri, and Bina D'Costa for great conversations. I would also like to thank my colleagues at Bangladesh Development Initiative, particularly Saad Andaleeb, Ahrar Ahmed, Munir Quddus, Farida Khan, Akhlaque Haque, and Elora Chowdhury for their interest in my work.

For help with interviews, I thank Yawar Harekar, Pushpita Alam, Sabir Mustafa, Tasbir Imam, Nadia Afrin, Kankana Mukhopadhyay, Awrup Sanyal, Alana Golmei, Mary Nukip, Sushovan Dhar, Meghna Guhathakurta, Mobashhar Alam Chowdhury, Rashed Sarwar, Anasua Ray, Prasenjit Kar, and my mother Shameem Subrana. For research assistance, I thank Takreem Siddiqui, Aninda Kumar Guha, and Julia Reilley at Colgate University and Sharmin Arzoo at the Shabab Murshid Development Foundation.

For reading and discussing the chapters with me, I thank my father K. A. S. Murshid, Nagesh Rao, Arafat Kazi, Sarah Grey, Alison Phillips, and Jalal

Alamgir, who is no longer with us. I thank Dorothea Schaefter and Jillian Morrison at Routledge for first advocating for me and then providing the necessary support throughout the writing process. I also thank the series editor, Subrata Mitra, for his support.

For travel and research grants, I thank the Major Grant (2010) and Discretionary Grants (2009–12) and the Colgate University Research Council—especially Judy Oliver and Lynn Staley.

For moral support and encouragement, I thank my family members and friends: Ma, Baba, Nadine, Dadubhai, Dadumoni, Nanu, Faisal, Tasdiq, Unzila, Fazabi, Alavi, Sabine, Fareen, Rameen, Tanhim, Nadia, Sadia, Nafisa, Saiq'a, Dina, Nayeem, Faheem, Shakib, Taposhda, Nitadi, Kuhelidi, Ahmedda, Himi, Joy, Lekhan Bhai, Keya Apa, Faarzein, Shayan, Pusha, Shima Apa, Aleef, Zaeem Bhai, Khadija, Pushpita, Safiya, Roohi, Wenjie, Malika, and Saretta. I also thank my students at Colgate University for providing a steady stream of inspiration during the last three years that I've been in Hamilton.

Above all, I thank and express gratitude to all those who have allowed me into their homes and lives and shared with me stories from some of the darkest times of their lives. I am humbled by their kindness, their strength, and their ability to smile in the face of adversity.

Abbreviations

AL	Awami League
BJP	Bharatiya Janata Party
BNP	Bangladesh Nationalist Party
BSF	Border Security Force
CBI	Central Bureau Investigation (India)
CNF	Chin National Front
CPM	Communist Party of India-Marxist
CPML	Communist Party of India (Marxist-Leninist)
CRC	Chin Refugee Committee
FAO	Food and Agriculture Organization
FRRO	Foreigner Regional Registration Office
GDP	Gross Domestic Product
IGO	International Governmental Organization
IMF	International Monetary Fund
IPKF	Indian Peace Keeping Force (in Sri Lanka)
ISI	Inter Services Intelligence (Pakistan's intelligence agency)
LTTE	Liberation Tigers of Tamil Eelam
MOH	Ministry of Health (Bangladesh)
MOU	Memorandum of Understanding
MP	Member of Parliament
MQM	Muhajir/Muttahida Quami Movement
MSF	Médicins Sans Frontières (Doctors Without Borders)
NAM	Non-aligned Movement
NATO	North Atlantic Treaty Organization
NGO	Non-governmental Organization
NLD	National League for Democracy
NSI	National Security Intelligence (Bangladesh's intelligence agency)
PM	Prime Minister
PML	Pakistan Muslim League
PML-N	Pakistan Muslim League—Nawaz Sharif faction
PPP	Pakistan People's Party
PTI	Pakistan Tehreek-e-Insaf

RAB	Rapid Action Bureau (Bangladesh's paramilitary force)
RAW	Research and Analysis Wing (India's intelligence agency)
RI	Refugees International
RSO	Rohingya Solidarity Organization
TULF	Tamil United Liberation Front
TYC	Tibetan Youth Congress
UN	United Nations
UNHCR	United Nations High Commission for Refugees
USCRI	United States Committee for Refugees and Immigrants
WHO	World Health Organization

1   Introduction

Immigration Officer, Dhaka, Bangladesh: Refugees? Aren't we all refugees in one way or another?

Immigration Officer, Kolkata, India: Refugees? There are lots of refugees in Assam. You should go there.

> (On hearing that my research is on the subject of refugees, while en route from Dhaka to Kolkata, December 14, 2012)

In the summer of 2012 Bangladesh made headlines by sealing its borders to ward off the Rohingya fleeing attacks in Myanmar, Indian politicians blamed "illegal immigrants" from Bangladesh for stirring ethnic violence in Assam, and Pakistan continued to harbor the largest refugee population in the world. Suddenly, it seemed that the silence had been broken, as refugee crises in South Asia rarely get international media attention, although many have been ongoing for decades. Academic research on these population groups is also limited and infrequent. Refugees play a crucial role in both domestic and international politics, yet much of the literature on South Asian politics focuses on corruption, Islamic fundamentalism, nuclear proliferation, regime change, and political instability.

Refugee populations in South Asia

Modern South Asia is the product of the partition of British India by colonial powers, one of the largest mass migration and refugee-creating events in history. The borders were drawn based on the Radcliffe Report commissioned by the British government. On July 18, 1947 the British Parliament passed the Indian Independence Act, which stipulated which provinces would be accorded to India and which to the newly created state of Pakistan. The creation of Pakistan was based on the premise that Hindus and Muslims living in the subcontinent constituted two different nationalities and could not coexist; Muhammad Ali Jinnah stepped down from Congress and joined the Muslim League in order to ensure a political space for Muslims that was mutually exclusive from that of the Hindus (James 2000). Whether it was the failure of

Congress and the Muslim League to reach consensus over power-sharing or the Machiavellianism of the British that created the grounds for Partition, India was divided, with repercussions that would continue to be felt for years to come.

Some viewed the creation of Pakistan as a way for the Indian Muslim minority to escape the problems of discrimination, underrepresentation, and hostility. However, Partition did little to resolve these issues in postcolonial India or Pakistan. The riots and the population exchanges that followed Partition left the remaining Muslims in India weak in number and political influence (T. M. Murshid 1995). Over the years India would witness the rise of a self-serving Hindu nationalism that identified Muslims as the "other," whose loyalty was suspect and who would be labeled as "refugees" from Pakistan and Bangladesh in a bid both to marginalize them and to bolster Hindu nationalism. In Pakistan, too, sectarian and ethnic violence continued; the empowerment envisioned by Jinnah left much to be desired. Ismailis and Ahmadiyas were declared non-Muslims owing to doctrinal differences. Shi'a–Sunni tensions flared up periodically. In West Pakistan, Balochis and Sindhis resented the Punjabi domination of politics, the army, and business—a resentment that persists today. The Biharis who entered East Pakistan during Partition were closely identified with the Punjabi pursuit of non-Bangali[1] domination, and there too one could identify anti-Punjabi sentiment. The situation was ripe for the development of ethnic tensions that eventually led to the break-up of Pakistan, during which ten million refugees fled to India. Afterward, 500,000 Biharis were left behind in Bangladesh as "stranded Pakistanis." One-half of these continue to live in squalid camps, waiting to be repatriated to Pakistan, even though they have been granted citizenship by the Bangladeshi government. Partition created more problems than it had resolved.

Sadly, those who migrated to the newly formed nation-states in 1947 are still identified as "refugees" in both India and Pakistan, especially if they are poor and of low caste;[2] the passage of over half a century has been insufficient for "integration." Following independence, all three countries—India, Pakistan, and Bangladesh—have had to host refugees from neighboring countries (see Table 1.1). However, it is only recently that our attention has begun to turn to the victims of many of these crises, thanks to aggressive state action against such vulnerable groups. Every communal conflagration, every riot, every state-sponsored pogrom—and there are many that blot South Asia's blood-soaked history—swells the numbers affected by a crisis that goes unnoticed by scholars and media pundits alike.

In turn, refugees have impacted states, policies, and politics more dramatically than one might imagine. States have used refugees as vote banks, as scapegoats to create national unity, as justification for military action at home and abroad—in short, as political pawns. Often rendered stateless, these populations might be said to exemplify the subaltern, whose representation in the political sphere is ruled out de facto and de jure. Unable to make claims

Table 1.1 Refugees from neighboring countries

Host and year	Refugee origin	Refugee population in the year of conflict	Refugee population in 2012	Notes
India				
2001	Afghanistan	11,972	13,200	
1997	Bangladesh (Indigenous)	64,000[1]	65,000	
1988	Bhutan	Unavailable	30,000	Diverted to Nepal
1959	China (Tibet)	80,000	100,000	
1972	Myanmar (Rohingya)	Unavailable	7,000–8,000	
1988	Myanmar (Chin)	Unavailable	86,000	
1947	Pakistan	8,000,000	200,000	
1971	Pakistan (Bangladesh)	9,000,000	Unavailable	
1983	Sri Lanka (Tamil)	134,053	73,000	
1989	Sri Lanka (Tamil)	122,000	73,000	
1995	Sri Lanka (Tamil)	55,062	73,000	
Pakistan				
1947	India	6,000,000–7,000,000	Unavailable	
1980[2]	Afghanistan	1,500,000	1,709,950	
2001	Afghanistan	2,197,821	1,709,950	
Bangladesh				
1971	Pakistan/India (Bihari)	50,000	250,000–300,000 (approx. 16,000 in camps)	
1978[3]	Myanmar (Rohingya)	200,000	229,900	
1984	Myanmar (Rohingya)	Unavailable	229,900	
1992	Myanmar (Rohingya)	270,000	229,900	
2012	Myanmar (Rohingya)	1,000[1]	229,900	

Sources: UNCHR 2005; UNCHR 2011; Amnesty International 2000; Minorities at Risk Project 2004; US Committee for Refugees and Immigrants 2009a, 2009b; *Times of India* 2011; Koo 2010; *Times of India* 2012; Sharma 2012; George 2011; Weiner 1993; Suryanarayan 2009; UNCHR 2002; Poppelwell 2007; UNCHR 2003, 2012a, 2012b, 2012c, 2012d, 2013; United Kingdom: Home Office 2011; Human Rights Watch 1996.
Notes:
1 This is not an end-of-year figure—this is the figure at the beginning of the year when the conflict was worse. Reuters puts the number between 50,000 and 60,000.
2 The Soviets invaded on December 24, 1979. It would be more meaningful to know how many were in Pakistan by the end of 1980.
3 The Nagamin rules became operational in 1977, which led to widespread abuse. The refugee population peaked in 1978 before they were shipped back to the Arakan.

of states, relying on the charity of NGOs, and counting on the goodwill of "host"[3] nations, they wait to return home.

South Asia provides a natural experimental framework for the study of host-refugee relations owing to the variation in its socioeconomic and political characteristics. India, Pakistan, and Bangladesh, despite their shared heritage and colonial experiences, are very different in terms of the political systems that they represent and the attitudes of the states. India, the world's largest democracy and the regional power, acts as a big bully just as frequently as it performs its "brotherly" duties. The Pakistani state remains a precarious democracy tethered to the military and one that is highly reliant on US aid for its survival. Bangladesh, despite a relatively better record of human development than India and Pakistan, remains one of the poorest and most densely populated countries in the world. Regardless of these differences, however, refugee populations in Bangladesh continue to live in wretched conditions. From time to time, protests erupt against conditions in the camps. The media express indignation and surprise, policy makers make promises, and the crisis fades. Such was the case in 1984 when protests broke out in the Refugee Camp for Stranded Pakistanis (popularly known as the Geneva Camp or the Bihari Camp) in Dhaka. The sympathy of international organizations operating there was short-lived, and the resulting sense of futility prevented camp dwellers from organizing to protest again.

However, the circumstances are not the same everywhere. In some instances protests flare up into armed conflict and refugees become militant. In others, engaging in armed conflict becomes the primary goal of camp dwellers. Violence, then, becomes the pretext for cracking down on refugees as host states turn hostile.

The rights of refugees

For all the talk of democracy and rights in South Asia—especially in the region's most powerful country, India—it is noteworthy that none of the three nations is a signatory to the 1951 Refugee Convention or its 1967 Protocol (UNHCR 2010). A quick glance at the Convention and Protocol relating to the Status of Refugees reveals how different the on-the-ground realities in South Asia are from the rights that international law affords refugees. According to the Convention, refugees have the right:

> not to be returned forcibly (*refouler*) to a sending country where the refugee has reason to fear persecution (Article 33);
> not to be expelled, except under certain conditions such as "danger to security" (Article 32);
> to freedom of religion (Article 4);
> to access courts and the judicial system (Article 16);
> not to be penalized for illegal entry into the host state (Article 31);
> to work (Article 17);
> to housing (Article 21);
> to (public) education (Article 22);
> to public relief, social welfare, and assistance (Article 23);
> to move freely within the territory (Article 26); and
> to be issued with identity cards and travel documents (Articles 27 and 28).

Most of these rights are denied to *encamped* refugees, let alone refugees outside of camps. Sadly, these rights are denied to citizens as well, which becomes the excuse and justification for the continued neglect of refugee communities. In effect, all three countries perform poorly when it comes to taking care of minority groups and the subaltern. That the concept of refugees is fluid and open to interpretation makes the provision of rights discriminatory. There follows a brief overview.

Legal status. As ethnicity is shared across borders, minorities within a state are often called "illegal immigrants." For example, India's Hindu right-wing party, the Bharatiya Janata Party (BJP), claims that the Bangali Muslims living in northeast India are actually "illegal immigrants" from Bangladesh, thereby justifying the local inhabitants' use of violence against them. Similarly, right-wing groups in Pakistan claim that the Hindu minorities there are in fact Indians. Therefore, even those who have a legal claim to protection from the state are not afforded these rights.

Work, housing, education. High levels of income inequality, joblessness, and abject poverty in low-income households preclude many in the region from even the basic necessities of life. Cities like Mumbai, Delhi, Karachi, and Dhaka are as much slum cities as they are metropolises. In fact, much of the anti-refugee sentiment emanates from the poor, who feel that refugee camps are in much better condition than their own places of abode—as they often include schools and hospitals, for example.

Social welfare. Locals point to the social welfare provisions for their own communities versus those made available to refugees to demonstrate that refugees are actually better off. Table 1.2 shows the state allocations and UNHCR allocations for locals and refugees, respectively.[4] Indeed, such figures highlight a discrepancy between provisions for citizens and refugees, but what they do not reveal is the high number of refugees who receive no support from the state or from international organizations. It is quite telling that of almost 200,000 refugees in India, UNHCR only "assists" 17,888, according to the *UNHCR India Factsheet 2012* (UNHCR 2012a).

Religious freedom. India and Bangladesh are constitutionally "secular" states, while Pakistan is an Islamic state. Hindus in Pakistan are discriminated against; Muslims in India, despite being a population of 150 million, remain politically disenfranchised and mosques are periodically attacked by Hindu fundamentalists with support from right-wing political parties. Bangladesh, owing to a national identity that highlights Bangali ethnicity rather than religion, allows for greater religious freedom, but even so is not immune to sectarian violence, as demonstrated by the attack on Hindu homes following the demolition in 1992 of the Babri Mosque in Gujarat, India. However, when the "other" religion coincides with a perception of refugee status, the conditions are far worse, as in the case of the Bangali Muslims in northeast India.

Access to courts. The courts in India, Bangladesh, and Pakistan are rife with corruption; many judges and lawyers can be bribed. Despite constitutional requirements for an independent judiciary, the de facto case is very different: people with political power can and do intervene in the decisions of the courts. Consequently, the rich, not the courts, are the purveyors of justice.

Table 1.2 Welfare spending per capita, citizens, and refugees

India	2012–13	2011–12	2010–11	2010–09	2008–09
Total social welfare spending budget* (millions of US dollars)	36,897.53	31,084.82	34,852.20	29,349.88	25,490.13
Population	1,190,863,679	1,207,740,408	1,224,614,327	1,241,491,960	1,195,495,000
Refugees	184,543	185,323	184,821	198,700	188,637
Per capita welfare budget (USD/person)	0.0000310	0.0000257	0.0000285	0.0000236	0.0000213
Per refugee welfare budget (USD/refugee)	0.1999400	0.1677332	0.1885727	0.1477095	0.1351280

Pakistan	2012–13	2011–12	2010–11	2010–09	2008–09
Total social welfare spending budget* (millions of US dollars)	44237.77138	37283.37079	37181.6913	33129.42564	30023.05085
Population	167,442,258	170,494,367	173,593,383	176,745,364	152,518,015
Refugees	1,780,935	1,740,711	1,900,621	1,702,670	1,706,200
Per capita welfare budget (USD/person)	0.0002642	0.0002187	0.0002142	0.0001874	0.0001968
Per refugee welfare budget (USD/refugee)	0.024839633	0.021418473	0.019562917	0.019457338	0.017596443

Bangladesh	2012–13	2011–12	2010–11	2010–09	2008–09
Total social welfare spending budget* (millions of US dollars)	5,235.50	4,599.24	4,916.34	4,364.94	3,809.08
Population	145,478,300	147,030,145	148,692,131	150,493,658	180,778,315
Refugees	28,389	228,586	229,253	229,130	229,671
Per capita welfare budget (USD/person)	0.0000360	0.0000313	0.0000331	0.0000290	0.0000211
Per refugee welfare budget (USD/refugee)	0.18419856	0.020120404	0.021445058	0.019050037	0.01658951

Source: Government and UNHCR Budgets 2008–2013, available at: www.unhcr.org/pages/49c3646c4b8.html.
Note: * Included items: General Education, Technical Education, Medical and Public Health, Family Welfare, Water Supply and Sanitation, Housing, Urban Development, Information.
For information on refugee populations and spending in 2012, I referred to the sections on India, Bangladesh, and Pakistan on the UNHCR website. For information on refugee populations from 2006–11, I referred to the 2011 UNHCR Global Reports for India, Bangladesh, and Pakistan.

Freedom of movement. There is freedom of movement under the law, of course. However, discrimination and sectarianism are barriers to mobility. During 2012 hundreds of Muslims who traveled to cities such as Mumbai and Bangalore to escape the violence in Assam fled these cities, too, because Hindu fundamentalists threatened to kill them if they stayed on longer; the police opened fire on a peaceful demonstration in Mumbai to show support for these victims. The clear message to the Assamese is "Stay in Assam—don't roam around." Xenophobia is not reserved for people from other countries; people from different districts fall prey to the same kind of regionalism, reinforced once again by the fluid concepts of refugees and "others."

Identity cards. In 2000 Pakistan became the first among the three countries to institute national identity cards for all of its citizens. Bangladesh commenced an identity card program in 2007 and India in 2010. The process, in many respects, is incomplete and even controversial, with allegations of "non-citizens" being issued with national identity cards in order to create vote banks for parties in power. In a region fraught with concerns and contentions about identity, identity cards are a way of further discriminating against the subaltern.

In an environment where identity has become a political issue, refugees have little protection under the law. Treated as "illegal immigrants" in most cases, these victims of circumstance have virtually no rights. In India, the Foreigners Act of 1946, together with its 2004 amendment, is the statute that provides for refugee rights. The 2004 amendment essentially allows authorities to detain "illegal immigrants." Bangladesh does not have a specific legal framework to deal with refugees either; the UNHCR notes that "in the absence of a national refugee law, UNHCR conducts refugee status determination (RSD) of urban asylum-seekers in Dhaka." Similarly to India, the Foreigners Act of 1946 and the Control of Entry Act of 1952 regulate foreigners and entry into Bangladesh, but do not explicitly mention refugees or give them special considerations.[5] Pakistan, too, does not make explicit provisions for refugees or their rights. "The core protection challenge in Pakistan is the absence of a specific legal regime for the protection of refugees," according to the UNHCR. It provides prima facie recognition of refugees and some legal provisions for them through specific agreements with the UNHCR and/or the Afghan government. The absence of local laws pertaining to refugees creates a culture of outward ad hoc-ism as well as incentives for the strategic manipulation of refugees.

As has been suggested thus far, even the definition of a "refugee" in the South Asian context is problematic. The epigraph to this chapter bears testimony to the fluidity of the meaning of the word. It appears to be a derogatory term that people use to identify those who do not "belong." Otherwise how can migrants from the Partition era still be referred to as refugees?[6] Why are the "stranded Pakistanis" in Bangladesh refugees? Stateless populations, of which there are several in South Asia, create another layer of complexity since they, too, are refugees. Therefore, the definition of a refugee, according to Article 1 of the 1951 Convention, as someone who "is outside his [or her] country of nationality" or "habitual residence"; has a "well-founded fear of being persecuted for reasons of race, religion, nationality, membership of a particular social group or political opinion"; and "is unable or ... unwilling to avail himself [or herself] of the protection of that country ... or, owing to such fear, is unwilling to return to it," does not necessarily apply in the South Asian context. In many cases, there is no "country of nationality" or "habitual residence" to which people can return, and yet they are deemed to be refugees!

Marginalized and lacking social, political, and economic power, refugees find themselves relying on receiving states, on the one hand, and facing up to an increasingly hostile host population on the other. Often the receiving state justifies the refugees' dire conditions as inevitable considering the poverty in their own country. The state may even find the "refugee burden" sufficiently great to justify military intervention.

Why this book?

Refugees have received little scholarly attention; in the political science literature they are most often treated as a by-product of civil wars. Since the end of the Cold War, much research has been carried out on civil wars; the post-Cold War era has been marked more by civil wars than by inter-state wars (Bennett and Stam 1996; Kaufmann 1996; Doyle and Sambanis 2000; Elbadawi and Sambanis 2002; Fearon and Laitin 2003; Fearon 2004; Collier and Hoeffler 2004; and so on). Accordingly, very little work has been published on refugees' political motivations, except in the popular media, which treats them either as helpless victims of conflict[7] or as dangerous and destabilizing forces, even terrorists (Zolberg et al. 1989; Dowty and Loescher 1996; Barber 1997; Adelman 1998; Terry 2002; Lischer 2003; Salehyan and Gleditsch 2006; Salehyan 2008). It is this victim-or-terrorist dichotomy against which I argue by showing, in Chapter 3, that refugees, despite being voiceless, paradoxically engage in protests, and in Chapter 4, that they are not terrorists threatening the national security of the state they are in, but rather are agents of political change in their country of origin.

It is in the above context that I examine refugees' proclivity to mobilize in order to demand change and argue that refugees are neither voiceless nor terrorists, and that this dichotomy is a convenient state-centric construct that snatches away refugees' agency and further marginalizes them. Are refugees sufficiently organized to act as a political entity? Are they "violent," as the popular media would have us believe? The literature on contentious politics (see, for example, the works of Tarrow (1994, 2011), Tilly (2005), and McAdam et al. (2001, 2008)) affords an initial theoretical basis for understanding the mobilization of refugees, showing that refugee groups have high cohesion to begin with, owing to their shared experience, making collective action easier than it might be under situations where solidarity needs to be built, but falls short of explaining why the voiceless actually exercise their voices!

I define protests as peaceful demonstrations that are generally geared toward making demands in some form. The Rohingya population in Bangladesh, for example, often mobilizes in order to demand working rights and the ability to move away from the campgrounds. For the coding process, I looked for information pertaining to demonstrations where refugees did not use weapons, although it may well be that local authorities clamped down on such demonstrations through the use of force.

In contrast to protests, I depict militarization as the process of the proliferation of arms and weapons in refugee camps. This conceptualization is somewhat problematic because militarization need not occur in refugee camps per se. Given that forms of militarization are often covert, it is difficult to identify non-refugee camp militarization until it is exposed by the media or until someone is willing to divulge that information. Therefore, in terms of the dataset I compiled, militarization outside refugee camps is likely to be underrepresented; I focus on refugee camp militarization only.

I argue that assertions that refugees are terrorists serve state interests and the perpetuation of hate politics and form the pretext for marginalization when, in fact, militancy and militarization among refugees occur only when the state is complicit. Without state support and patronage, I argue, it is suicidal for refugee groups to engage in militancy, especially in the context of protracted refugee crises where so much is at stake, as is the case in South Asia.

State perspectives are more extant in the literature. Schweitzer et al. (2005), O'Rourke and Sinnott (2006), and Kessler et al. (2010) are among those who study attitudes toward refugees and conclude that such perceptions are often negative. Hernes and Knudsen (1992), Clark and Legge (1997), Fetzer (2000), Mayda (2006), and Hainmueller and Hiscox (2010) talk about attitudes toward refugees as well, although their main focus is on inter-group dynamics and attitudes toward immigrants.

However, the problem is that most of these studies are based on developed countries that are also advanced democracies, such as the United States, Australia, Germany, and the Netherlands, making it questionable whether such findings apply to developing countries as well. First, in less advanced countries, attitudes are likely to be far more negative because of higher competition over limited resources, especially in cases where refugees are able to obtain jobs (officially or illegally). Second, the "political nature" of refugees in the developing world differs from that found in advanced countries because (1) advanced countries have well-developed, institutionalized mechanisms for refugee integration, and (2) advanced countries are rarely countries of first asylum and are therefore protected from "sudden shocks," which precludes the need for active acts of political participation such as protests in order to address refugee issues. Yet developing countries rank among the top refugee-receiving countries in the world, according to the UNHCR Global Report.[8]

What does not vary with the level of development is the anti-refugee stance that states often take. Why are governments often anti-refugee? There is a small but growing literature that focuses on the social impact of refugee camps, which in turn can impact government policies regarding refugees. Chaulia (2003), for example, points out that traditionally Tanzania was friendly toward refugees, but since the 1990s Tanzania no longer operates an open-door policy. While some (like Chaulia) argue that the change has been associated with trade liberalization, others such as Lischer (2005) purport that it was a result of the negative experience of hosting refugees for a long time. That negative experience was primarily due to the fact that the camps had become rebel bases for Rwandan refugees; the refugees posed a serious threat to law and order, especially near camp areas. There were also fears that locals could be recruited into these groups and that civil war would be imported along with the refugees. With limited capacity to control the camps, it was easier to close the borders and decide whether refugees could enter the country on a case-by-case basis.

Lischer is not alone in identifying militarization as a reason for which states can harbor anti-refugee sentiments. Scholars such as Zolberg et al. (1989), Lake and Rothchild (1998), Mamdani (2002), Loescher et al. (2008), and Salehyan (2008) argue that camp militarization occurs because refugees often remain in camps for years, since receiving states and the international community can rarely offer them a better option. States perceive refugees located in camps as sources of insecurity because camps often harbor or create transnational rebels or terrorist movements. Accordingly, refugee camps become epicenters of regional conflict because these rebels exploit or manipulate refugees to further their own ends when other actors are complacent or even supportive (Stedman and Tanner 2003; Loescher and Milner 2005; Loescher et al. 2008).

This stream of literature seems to delegitimize the demands of refugees in terms of political change in the country of origin. As refugees sometimes use aid money to finance separatist movements, scholars such as Fiona Terry (2002) argue that the aid regime should come to an end. Such recommendations, however, ignore the political contexts that give rise to refugee situations in the first instance. Would a separatist movement with strong leaders and firm resolve, for example, fizzle out without access to aid? In such cases, greater focus, perhaps, should be placed on resolving the political crises that give rise to separatist movements. This line of argument also suggests that anti–home state behavior is illegitimate because it is influenced by "greed" (Collier 1999; Collier and Hoeffler 2004). Although in the case of natural resources—oil, diamonds, ivory, gold—greed has spurred violent conflicts (Collier 1999; Ross 2004), such generalizations do not hold in the South Asian context because no such resources exist. Instead, a history of colonization, decolonization, partition, migration, and a fluid concept of "homeland" explains much of the demand for separatism.

Closing borders is a low-cost option that Bangladesh currently employs on its eastern border, preventing the Myanmar Rohingya from entering the country to join the half-million official and unofficial refugees already in Bangladesh. Unlike in 1971, when India found its solution to the refugee crisis of ten million Bangalis fleeing genocide in what was then East Pakistan in the form of a military intervention to "liberate Bangladesh," Bangladesh has neither the military nor diplomatic power to force a solution on Myanmar. In such situations, closing borders allows the receiving state to be "aggressive" without the potential diplomatic repercussions.

This brings us to the actual use of force in resolving refugee crises. Traditionally, the literature treats intervention as an instrument of foreign policy. For example, Morgenthau (1967) and Rosenau (1967) both depict intervention as a tool in the pursuit of foreign policy goals. On the one hand, intervention is a coercive strategy undertaken by the intervener to undermine the authority of the target government. On the other, interventions are costly and require large amounts of resources. Thus, the traditional view is that intervention is a tool that wealthier countries wield (Morgenthau 1967; Rosenau 1967; Bull 1984; Krasner 1999; Dorman and Otte 1995).

By focusing on South Asia, I depart from this traditional understanding of intervention by explaining why it may be undertaken by countries that do not meet the "wealthy" criterion, and positing intervention as a tool of domestic policy. I argue that refugees are not merely a negative consequence of civil wars, but that they can impact policies and politics. No longer can the study of refugees be solely a topic for liberals arguing for humanitarianism in international politics.

Instead, I argue that refugees can create situations that are counter to the national interests of the states in which they take refuge, whereby they are forced to respond in a "realist" fashion. It is from this conceptualization of refugees that I study the case of India's intervention in Bangladesh's War of Independence. I rely on the premise that countries intervene militarily in their neighboring refugee-sending countries not necessarily as a result of malicious intent, but because they are forced to do so given the anarchic international structure apparent from the reluctance of other actors (the United Nations, for example) to get involved. The cost of maintaining refugees becomes so high that it is in the interest of the receiving state to intervene militarily in the refugee-sending country. The idea of military interventions is contentious primarily because of the implications for state sovereignty. According to the UN Charter, neither a state nor the UN can infringe on another state's sovereignty. Self-defense is the only justification that states have for the use of force. The question is: when there is a large refugee population residing in a country, does military intervention in the refugee-sending country count as an act of self-defense? A key gap in our understanding of refugee-host interaction is the political nature of their existence.

Are refugees marginalized, voiceless, and thus in need of charity, as some of the human rights literature suggests? Or are they terrorists and rebel warriors, as some of the political science literature proposes? The reality is somewhere in between. Is this dichotomy, then, a state-centric construct that serves to marginalize refugees perpetually? How have states dealt with refugees? This book will tackle these issues in light of the grim realities of the refugee crises in India, Pakistan, and Bangladesh and make the case that, ultimately, state interests and state manipulation of refugees perpetuate and sustain the protracted nature of the crises.

Methodology

This book uses a mixed-method approach to respond to the questions posed above. The analyses presented in the chapters on protest and militarizations are based on an original dataset created using newspaper reports of protests, arms dealings, and violence among refugees. It contains annual data from 1950 to 2012 (1971 to 2012, in the case of Bangladesh) for each of the refugee groups in India, Pakistan, and Bangladesh. For each refugee group (such as the Rohingya) I have collected annual data for the entire period during which they were refugees. Details of the data are given in Appendix 1. I also conducted interviews to supplement the quantitative analysis, given the limitations of media-generated data.

For Chapter 2 I interviewed various types of refugees living in India, Pakistan, and Bangladesh. In India and Bangladesh I interviewed refugees in camps, camp areas, public places, or in their places of abode or work, depending on individual circumstances. In some cases they were randomly selected. In others local NGOs directed me to certain refugee areas. In Pakistan I contacted refugees through formal and informal contacts.

The analysis presented in Chapter 3 and Chapter 4 was supplemented by the following interviews:

- Bihari refugees in the Refugee Camp for Stranded Pakistanis in Dhaka (Bangladesh)
- Rohingya refugees in Cox's Bazar (Bangladesh)
- Bangali refugees who returned to Bangladesh (Khulna and Dhaka) from India following the liberation of Bangladesh
- Chin refugees in West Delhi (India)
- Tibetan refugees in North Delhi (India)
- Afghan refugees in Peshawar (Pakistan)
- Afghan returnees from Pakistan in Kabul (Afghanistan)
- Freedom fighters from Bangladesh's Liberation War in Dhaka (Bangladesh)
- Tamil Sri Lankan refugees in Bangalore (India)
- Activists and aid workers in (1) refugee camps in Kutapolong and Nayapara, Cox's Bazar, Bangladesh; (2) refugee villages in Rawalpindi, Pakistan; and (3) Delhi, India.

For Chapter 5 I relied on secondary material as well as interviews with aid practitioners and aid workers to provide evidence for my arguments. For Chapter 6 I used archival research and surveys to provide an in-depth understanding of the reasons for India's intervention. More specifically, I consulted primary documents held at the National Archives in Delhi from the time of the intervention (1971), such as speeches given in Parliament; I interviewed freedom fighters in Bangladesh; and I surveyed Indians and Bangladeshis who lived in refugee camps and camp areas in India during the 1971 war.

Summary

The book argues that refugees have agency when it comes to exercising their right to a better lifestyle, but are also susceptible to state manipulation. It is state interests and state politics that eventually dictate how refugees will fare in any given country. The central argument of the book thus rests upon a criticism of the state and of ad hoc, state-centric refugee policies. The Chronology provides an easy template through which to assess occasions when state policies and politics have coincided with refugee creation and protection.

In writing about refugees, refugee policies, and state responses, it is often easy to forget that we are actually discussing people—individuals—whose lives have been upturned, perhaps forever, by war, famine, or natural disasters that have forced them to seek refuge in a foreign country, where they are at the mercy of the kindness of strangers. It is also easy to analyze interactions between refugees and the state in a very abstract form. In an attempt to humanize the subject at hand—namely the politics of refugees—and to put a human face in front of the theories and evidence presented here, I begin with personal stories of refugees spread across South Asia in Chapter 2.

Chapter 3 theorizes and analyzes the "audacity" of refugees, who have no rights within any state structure, to engage in protests in an attempt to change the course of their lives. It provides evidence to counter the "victim" characterization of refugees and shows that despite all markers of "victimhood," refugees have agency and exercise voice to protest their marginalization—especially when they are supported by locals who can use their rights as citizens to advocate for refugees. I show that the main state-related factors influencing protests are safety, protection, and living conditions—factors that the state and/or international organizations control.

Chapter 4, then, counters the characterization of refugee groups as "terrorist," arguing that instances of refugee camp militarization are the product of separatist elements among refugees and, more importantly, the support of the receiving state itself in the South Asian context. I argue that it is only when the state is complicit, explicitly or implicitly, that refugees can become militants or "refugee warriors." Empirical analysis based on the same dataset as Chapter 3 provides evidence to show that the militarization of refugee camps is a function of state support, explicit or implicit, which means that states can prevent militarization if they have the will to do so, and that the incentive for militarization need not come from the refugees themselves—the state is the ultimate player.

Owing to the limitations of media-generated data, Chapter 5 provides a descriptive analysis of the different refugee groups in the region and shows how the state manipulates refugee groups to serve domestic, regional, and international interests. I argue that states have an agenda that is motivated by material gains and nationalist propaganda.

India's intervention in Bangladesh's War of Independence is perceived by many as a humanitarian one. In fact, it is, perhaps, the only instance of humanitarian intervention to be undertaken by a South Asian nation. Chapter 6 examines the degree to which the military intervention of 1971 can be characterized as humanitarian and argues that refugees provided the pretext for an intervention that resulted in India firmly establishing its position as a dominant player in regional politics. Chapter 7 concludes with the question of whether there can be a state-based solution to statelessness and refugee crises.

Notes

1 Instead of using the English word "Bengali" to denote both the language and the ethnicity, I use the local terms "Bangla" and "Bangali" to denote the language and the ethnicity, respectively.

2 There are labels, too: Muslims from India who migrated to Pakistan are called "Muhajir" in Pakistan; Bangalis from Muslim parts of Bengal (East Bengal, now Bangladesh) who migrated to India are called "Bangal" in India.

3 The literature identifies the refugee-receiving countries as "host states." I refrain from using this terminology as much as possible because the receiving states rarely act as hosts. The refugees are neither guests nor parasites; hence, the receiving state can hardly be deemed a host.

4 Different countries define social welfare according to the size of their budgets. The metric I use includes traditional social safety nets, such as education (including technical education) and healthcare spending.

5 There are some articles in Bangladesh's Constitution which might, in theory, guarantee the protection of refugee rights. However, they are not observed in practice. Relevant provisions include: "support oppressed people throughout the world waging a just struggle against imperialism, colonialism and racism" (Article 24(1) (c)); the obligation to "base its international relations on the principles and respect for international law and the principles enunciated in the UN Charter" (Article 25); the obligation to protect every citizen and "every other person within Bangladesh for the time being" (Article 31); and the obligation that "no person shall be deprived of life and liberty save in accordance with the law" (Article 32).

6 There is certainly a class element, however. The rich and educated are not called refugees. Some Partition migrants now occupy high positions in society, and are senior government officials or politicians, for example. This includes the current prime minister, Manmohan Singh, who is hardly likely to be called a refugee!

7 For examples see the *Journal of Refugee Studies* and *International Migration Review,* the two leading journals on refugee issues; much of the work that they publish focuses on the trauma and welfare provisions relating to refugees in different parts of the world.

8 The only countries that have resettlement programs are Australia, Austria, Belgium, Canada, Denmark, France, Germany, the Netherlands, Norway, Spain, Sweden, Switzerland, the United Kingdom, and the United States. Hosting refugees is a challenge and takes place on a more ad hoc basis in most other countries.

2   Refugee voices

When considering refugees in the context of conflicts, it is often easy to forget that we are talking about individuals. Their voices are overshadowed by an abstract idea of state-refugee relations. Thus, before I proceed to analyze refugees as political actors and political tools—that is, before I run the risk of presenting them as forward-looking, rational actors—I will present some of their personal stories. On the one hand, their geographic location means very little: the stories can be from anywhere. On the other hand, the very fact that they are in specific geographic locations means that they are subject to country-specific laws, regulations, and manipulation; it actually matters whether the state is a rising power, for example. Their stories need no analysis; on their own, they send powerful messages of struggle, of agency, of perseverance, and of survival. The careful reader will note that the Tibetan story is very different from the Chin story, and the Bihari story is very different from the Rohingya story, even though the "host" state is the same. It is only by keeping in mind the on-the-ground realities of refugees' individual lives that the analyses presented in this book can have any impact on how we think about refugees and about resolving refugee crises.

Sima Begum

Bihari refugee
Forty-five years old
Rehabilitation Camp for Stranded Pakistanis (Geneva Camp)
Mohammadpur, Dhaka, Bangladesh
October 17, 2012

We've been here since the *gondogol*[1] of March 25, 1971. This is our own room. It has always been that. My mother used to live here, my brothers used to live here. I got married here, I had three children here. I live here. My daughters are eighteen and fifteen years old; my son died soon after he was born.

My husband left me and remarried, so I remained here with my mother and children. My brothers are now busy with their wives and children. My mother died three years ago and left this room for us. If I had money, I could build more floors here, but I don't.

My children attend the government school nearby, but it's expensive—we need to pay examination fees. In the camp school, it is all free. I will start sending my younger daughter to that school next year.

We speak Hindi and Bangla. Thanks to Allah, we speak two languages. I am a *dal-khichuri*,[2] my mother Bangali, my father Bihari. I can pass as both. Thanks to the popularization of Hindi films, I am considered exotic. Many people outside the camp say, "Teach us Hindi!"

We became Bangladeshi citizens when the government gave us permission. But we continue to live in the camp. Some have tried to live outside the camp, but most of them came back because of the many benefits here. See, I have two fans, two fridges, and lights in this room, and I don't have to pay for it. I don't have to pay any utility bills, nor any rent. Where else in Dhaka would I find this?

We do not face any discrimination here. Everyone treats us well. Bangalis actually come and rent rooms in the camp because it is so cheap here. Some families who have more than one room often rent out rooms. Some Bangalis who come to rent speak Bihari Hindi so well that that you won't be able to tell they are Bangali! So there is no chance that they look down upon us. Otherwise, why would they want to come and live here with us?

Still, there are some who leave the camp—people who leave for Pakistan, people who marry Bangalis and live in the city, those who want to build a better future. My brother married someone in Dhaka and left the camp. He is a car mechanic now. It's good work.

Before, I used to think Nasim Khan [the refugee coordinator] would take us to Pakistan. My mother, on her deathbed, told me, "Go get your identity card. Don't wait for Pakistan. That will never happen." But my mother had really wanted to go to Pakistan. Her sister was in Karachi and she wanted to be with her. But we didn't have money and the Pakistani government never made any arrangements. She waited to go to Pakistan all her life, but in her dying days realized that that was not to be, that we had to make our lives in Bangladesh.

People just scream, "Pakistan, Pakistan!" What good would it do? Would people really benefit from going there? I have no desire to go there anymore. When I was a child, I wanted to go, but not anymore. This camp is my home now.

Today, I work as domestic help in a house. My older daughter works as a maid too. My youngest daughter is still in school. Until she gets married, we want her to continue school and prevent her from having to work as a maid.

These days I am busy with wedding arrangements for my older daughter Shanta. I want my daughters to stay close by. But Shanta's fiancé doesn't want to come live in the camp. I hope he reconsiders. He can rent a room here. But my daughter doesn't communicate this to him.

In any case, whatever lies in her path will happen. I haven't placed restrictions on whom she can marry—a Bangali, a Hindu, a Bihari—as long as she is happy and as long as he is a good man. Money is a little important, but money can't buy happiness and I would rather have my daughter be happy.

Raju

Deported Pakistani
Thirty-five years old
Rehabilitation Camp for Stranded Pakistanis (Geneva Camp)
Mohammadpur, Dhaka, Bangladesh
October 17, 2012

When I was ten years old, I remember boarding a plane for the first time in my life. That was a life-changing plane ride because overnight my home was transformed from Dhaka to Karachi. My mother, my seven sisters, and my three brothers were with me. I was the youngest. We landed in Karachi where my *chachajan* [father's brother] lived. He helped us to set up a home.

My father didn't come. He remained in Dhaka. We soon found out that he had married a Bangali woman there. We would speak to him on the phone every now and then, but I didn't see him again until twenty more years had gone by.

In Pakistan, we were part of the Muhajir community. The Muhajirs form a different group, like the Pathans, Punjabis, Balochs, and Sindhis. We had our own leader, Altaf Hussain, who represented us. We lived well. My father would send us money. The environment was very nice. There were many other Muhajirs.

I used to work at a garment factory. I met my wife there. We got married and had a child.

Although we obtained national identity cards, we never got passports since we never travelled. Five years ago, after I got married, my wife and I wanted to travel. I applied for a passport. The passport authorities said I was an illegal immigrant from Bangladesh and I had to be deported. I tried to explain that I had been living there since I was ten. My wife is Pakistani. I am a Pakistani too. The travel agent I was working with found me a good deal. The agent prepared my deportation papers and for only 25,000 rupees I was able to come to Bangladesh.

That was a difficult experience, but since my father was in Bangladesh, it was not as difficult as it could've been. It was thus that I was able to see my father again after being away for twenty years. I came to the Bihari camp and set up a mobile phone shop.

Everyone here is nice, but I am having trouble fitting in. My heart is still in Pakistan. I think the environment there is better. Part of the reason is that my Bangla is not very good. I can't speak it as fluently as a native. My wife speaks no Bangla at all and so it is difficult for her to go out very much. We plan on going back to Karachi next year. We will have to make an appeal to the Pakistani embassy. I hope they sort things out soon. I have had another child since coming back here. I would like to go back to Pakistan.

Mastura Ahmed Huq

Partition refugee from West Bengal
Mirpur, Dhaka, Bangladesh
Seventy-two years old
October 20, 2012

I was born in Murshidabad, my *nanabari* [maternal grandmother's home] in Taranagar *gram* [village]. I never met my father. When my mother was pregnant with me, my father became a nomad, forcing my mother to go and live with her parents. My early childhood days in Taranagar were beautiful in the midst of my mother's family—her six sisters whom I called *khalas* [mother's sisters], her parents, and a host of uncles and aunts and their families.

I remember everything being plentiful. Nana owned large amounts of land. He owned paddy fields, mustard fields, ponds, and farms. He wasn't a *zamindar* [landlord] but he owned a lot of land. They say you keep *dhaan* [unprocessed rice] in a *gola* [silo]. But there were no *golas*—the grain would be kept in barns with windows on top. We would climb in through the window using a ladder and swerve through the grains for a joyride. Our whole bodies would itch later on, but what fun!

I don't remember the circumstances under which this happened, but my mother started working at a refugee camp in Kolkata [India] in 1945. I don't remember where the people were from, but we called them refugees. Soon, however, riots broke out and we made a quick escape back to Murshidabad from Kolkata [in 1946]. Everyone in the family thought Murshidabad would become part of Pakistan.

Soon, of course, we realized that Murshidabad had been allocated to India. The home was abuzz with cries of surprise, sorrow, and regret. In time, I would hear my mother and her sisters talk about a place called Dhaka. Until then, Kolkata was the place to be. What was this Dhaka? To my surprise, my *boro khalu* [mother's oldest sister's husband] took up employment there. Slowly, my other *khalas* followed suit. They wanted to be in Pakistan.

We remained in Taranagar—my mother, sister, Godi Khala, and I in my *nanabari*. Things were no longer the same, however. No, it wasn't that our Hindu neighbors turned against us. It was our own family. Because my mother had female siblings only, my grandfather, under pressure from his family, had married again in the hope of a male heir. The family's wishes were granted: he had two sons who were about my age. So, when we returned to Murshidabad, my sister Rokeya and I were no longer the favored children; in fact, we became *chokher bali.*[3] But when my grandfather died in 1945, it was in my mother's bed. In his dying moments, he told his brothers to look after my Nani and to give my mother fifty *bighas* [about 12.5 acres) of land. But of course none of that happened. Instead, the house was partitioned in the middle: we got the front side of the house, the stairs to the roof, and an outside toilet, but not the courtyard, not the back of the house, not the well, nor the pond. At this point, we were still in Murshidabad.

Let me introduce another character at this point: Tunu Dada, my first cousin, the only son of my *boro khala,* who at the time was in Dhaka with his parents. He was a very bright kid, but he would have these psychotic episodes where he would go and lie next to an open drain for hours, or he would hallucinate that my father was calling him to become a nomad with him. Afraid that he would run away, my *khala* tied him up. It was during one such episode that Tunu Dada sent a letter to Nani in Murshidabad saying, "If you come to me, I will get better." Tunu Dada was the apple of Nani's eyes. Of course she had to go to Dhaka. We all went.

It was this trip to Dhaka that effectively made us homeless. When we came back, we saw our home had been broken into. My Nana's second wife, in alliance with his brothers, had taken over the entire house.

I remember vividly how Haroun Mama, my mother's cousin, had advocated for Nani's share in the property; how Nana's youngest brother Mansur Chacha brought Nani and Haroun Mama to meet Nana's other brothers to negotiate over the property, but instead tried to kill Haroun Mama by stabbing his chest with a hot arrow and by throwing acid on his back. I was young, but I remember being shocked and confused; I remember how I couldn't find Nani and feared that she had been killed. Eventually, it was the border guards and police who helped us—took me to Nani and all of us to Bahalampur, five stations away, where there was a hospital to treat Haroun Mama.

That day, Nani made a pact with Allah: if Haroun Mama lived, she would let go of her claim to the property. Haroun Mama lived and we said goodbye to Murshidabad.

My *khalas* in Dhaka helped Nani to buy a house in Chapainawabganj. Although it wasn't too bad, compared to the house in Taranagar, this house was cramped and old. It had fourteen rooms, but it also had snakes! Nani never complained, never talked about Taranagar again or about that house. But her sorrow was evident in her silence.

It is strange, is it not, that at a time when communal violence made people flee from their homes, in our case it was our relatives who took advantage of the political situation and literally made us homeless overnight? Unfortunately, there are others like us who became victims of people who took advantage of politics to "resolve" home politics.

I have to say, however, that Murshidabad was a relatively violence-free area, probably because it was a Muslim-majority district. My mother's half-brothers still live there, in apparent communal harmony. I will be visiting Murshidabad next month and taking a trip down memory lane. I do wonder what kind of a homecoming that will be!

Arshadul Mostafa

Thirty-eight years old
Rohingya refugee
Kutapalong Refugee Camp

Cox's Bazar, Bangladesh
October 21, 2012

I used live in Bodinagar. My family is there; I am here with my wife. I left in 1988 as a student of Class 8. I was part of the National Democratic Party and I had to leave. When [Aung San] Suu Kyi came from London, the public didn't let her go back to London. Many of us claimed we would commit suicide if she left! We felt she was the only one who could bring about change.

My father and brother were government officers. They made a pact with the Rakhine government—they gave the military land in exchange for protection. We have been living there for generations. I have documents to prove it, but the state does not accept my papers. Instead, the government gave us identity cards that said we were guests, with which we couldn't go even to the next village. It was only after coming to Bangladesh that we realized that we were like caged birds. We didn't know what democracy really was, what socialism really was.

When we first came, I was scared of all men in uniform because that is what we were used to. I used to run away. The level of torture in Myanmar was horrendous.

Myanmar is a rich state; it can produce enough to feed its people, even if it doesn't have friends. The government can utilize the state apparatus and its authority to create a well-functioning socialist state by dividing who should eat what. There is no value for land there. You can't sell land. You can hand it over, but not sell it. Sales take place in backhanded ways, through corruption. The land can be used for food production to prevent starvation.

Those who have family, relatives, friends—who wants to leave and live in a room made out of polythene bags? Would anyone choose such a life? No ethnic group has won against the military government, but for us, the question is one of nationality. The government doesn't want us to have Myanmarese nationality. They changed the name from Arakan to Rakhine State, denying our position there. Those who have citizenship can protest; how can we? We as a group are facing torture and violence even as I speak; villages are being burnt down.

In 1984 the government took away my nationality. We couldn't leave the house for fear. During the same time, the government demonetarized several bank notes, the possession of which then became punishable by law. On the one hand, we couldn't leave our homes for fear of being killed or tortured; on the other hand, remaining at home with demonetarized currencies carried a seven-year prison sentence. The Myanmar government was very strict.

It was literally *Mogher mulluk*.[4] The Moghs, the military's "civilian" allies, got away with everything, ruled everything in Arakan, and terrorized us.

After leaving Myanmar, people can't go back home because of the law—we need permits to go to the next state, so how can we cross the border? But if you have money you can bribe your way into Myanmar. The poor are unable to do so—there are checkpoints, the *gram bahini*, the Moghs, who could show up any time to harass us or to do a census count. If there are more people than reported in the census, the extra people will get arrested. They have the right to enter your home at any given time.

When I left in 1988, it was in the midst of political turmoil: the government opened the borders and said "Go hide where you can—we are giving you twenty-four hours." I didn't come to Bangladesh first—from Rangoon I went to Thailand. I was among lakhs of people who had left Myanmar at the same time.

UNHCR received us in Thailand. They registered us and put us up in hotels—many of us in one room—not just Rohingyas, but refugees of different ethnicities and nationalities. There was a lot of uncertainty in Thailand, and I faced discrimination there because I was a Muslim. I had an uncle in Karachi, Pakistan, and I decided to go live with him in a Muslim country.

But how to get to Karachi? My uncle directed me toward a hotel-cum-agent in Bangkok that apparently also served as a *dalal* [middleman]. The agent told me they would be able to get me a passport to travel. I thought it would take weeks if not months to arrange. In the meantime, I was running out of money. However, two days later, I had in my hands a Pakistani passport with my photograph but a different name. I boarded a plane bound for Karachi.

At immigration, I was sent from one officer to another. After several rounds, they let me in. I realized they were in on the "contract."

In 1992 we got news that many Rohingyas were fleeing to Bangladesh. I thought my family members would be among them. Some of my Rohingya friends there felt the same. We decided we had to go to Bangladesh. We consulted another *dalal*, who had a plan which sounded fantastical, but it worked.

First we obtained Pakistani nationality by buying a national ID card for 2,000 rupees and a passport for 1,500 rupees. We got an Indian visa on that passport, which was valid for three months. We took a train from Karachi to Lahore and then a bus to Delhi. In Delhi, we needed to register because we were officially Pakistani citizens, and Pakistanis have to register if they visit India. The *dalal* told us which address to use for registration. The registration allowed us to go anywhere within India within the three-month period. We didn't need so much time. We paid yet another *dalal* 2,000 rupees, which ensured safe transit from Delhi straight into Jessore here in Bangladesh. It was as though there were no international borders! That was in 1992, right after the cyclone in Chittagong.

I came to Cox's Bazar and realized that my family had not come. I registered with UNHCR here. I got married in 2005 to another Rohingya. We live in a shed in the camp with our two children. We are entitled to six kilograms of rice for fifteen days per person in the camp. If we measure it at home, it's five kilograms, though! It really isn't enough because we get no protein other than *dal* [lentils], but because I have an outside job, we get by.

Life is difficult. Officially, we can't leave the camps. We need permission even to come out to the tea stall outside. Even so, those of us in the camps are better off because we have protection. Those who are unregistered are the ones who are really vulnerable. They have no protection from aid agencies, nor do they get any sympathy from locals. Now that there is fresh violence in Myanmar there are many more unregistered refugees.

To a certain degree we can pass off as Bangladeshis, and many unregistered Rohingyas try to do that quite successfully. Our language is close to Chittagongian, but any Chittagongian speaker can tell that our language is different. We can't get away! It's safer to speak in proper Bangla because the locals and the Rohingyas speak the same level of proper Bangla. So it's actually more difficult for me to try and speak Chittagongian. Looks-wise, however, there really is very little difference, which makes it easy to blend in.

For myself, I have found a place as a photographer for now, but I don't know what the future holds. Where will the solution come from? We want Myanmar to give us back our citizenship, but Myanmar doesn't pay heed to anyone—not the USA, not the European Union. I became homeless for Suu Kyi, but Suu Kyi has no place for us either. The only hope now is the UN. But does the UN have the will to resolve our problems? I hope so.

Nu Ting

Chin Refugee
Forty-three years old
One of several tin shed rooms on the roof of a two-storey residence
Uttamnagar, Delhi, India
September 28, 2012

I was in Burma. My husband and I owned a convenience store where we sold food near an army camp in Sagian Division, just outside Chin state. Because we were near an army camp, most of our customers consisted of army personnel. They would help themselves to our products without paying. They would say they would pay later, but they never did. We tried to complain to the authorities, but the government paid no heed. Soon after, some army men robbed our village. When we filed an FIR [first investigative report], we were told to shut up if we wanted to live here. To make matters worse, the army filed a false case against my husband. I didn't even get to see him.

My husband had gone to the police station to check on our case. Soon after, a neighbor came running to me with the news of my husband's arrest. My husband apparently told the neighbor that he would try to escape, and that we should escape too. I never saw him again.

With our three young daughters—aged eleven, nine, and four—I made my way to a church in the next village and hid there. The next morning the church pastors dropped us off at the house of their missionary friends in the border town of Manipur [India]. The border is porous—people go back and forth all the time. There is no need for documents. So we just crossed over. That was in August 2008.

Although the crossing was easy, we weren't safe. There were periodic checks to send back "illegal immigrants," during which we had to hide. We were advised to go to Delhi, the only place where UNHCR has offices.

It was a scary journey; paradoxically, more scary than fleeing Burma. We didn't know the language; we were hungry but didn't know the names of the food here, and only ate biscuits for three days. My four-year-old was sick throughout and kept throwing up. I felt like I would collapse. In that almost-unconscious state, I remember that it was the kindness of strangers that made me move forward. Unfortunately, I don't remember who they were or what they were called.

We found our way to Old Janakpuri, where we were met by a Burmese family. Their room was too small to fit us all in, so we slept under the open sky on the roof. My daughters didn't understand why we had to leave our own big house in Burma to come and live here like this. They were homesick and wanted to go back.

We registered with UNHCR office here, but I couldn't find a proper job. I followed some other Chin women and started working at a garment factory, only to find out at the end of the month that I would get 1,000 rupees for the month's work instead of the 2,500 rupees we had agreed on. I complained to the UNHCR representatives, but they said the law would not help us because we are not allowed to work; we are working illegally.

Now I have found work through Don Bosco's microfinance program, which has allowed me to purchase a knitting machine on monthly installments. Don Bosco provides me with wool, and I make sweaters and get thirty rupees per sweater. Still, life is difficult.

My children are fifteen, thirteen, and eight now. Only the youngest one can go to school, because she has a sponsor. The other two have had no education since we arrived here. The culture here is very crude and the men are disrespectful. Only last night I sent my fifteen-year-old to get some milk from the store just around the corner. A few minutes later she ran back home crying—some men had just walked up to her and started fondling her breasts. I have three daughters and I live in constant fear.

It seems like no one can help us. The Chin Refugee Committee and UNHCR have limited powers. I wish I could go back home. There is talk of democracy, but what does that mean? I don't know what to believe.

In Burma, we had everything. It is a beautiful country. The air is fresh. The water is sweet. Here, we need to walk a mile to get fresh water. The water in the tap is salty. The army has done terrible things, but in general people are nice and friendly. Peace in Burma is linked to my peace of mind.

Here, I have no future, no hope. My children are my only hope, my only strength. My children and God. I am leaving everything to God because I have no other choice. I don't know what awaits me.

Tenzing Ho Kad

Tibetan refugee born in India
Thirty-five years old
Tibetan Refugee Colony

New Aruna Nagar, New Delhi, India
October 6, 2012

I was born in Darjeeling in 1977, but I have no memory of it. My father was a Tibetan government officer working for the Finance Department, and that meant frequent transfers. When I was about three, my father was transferred to Rajpur, then Delhi, then Gangtok, and then back to Delhi. That is where my childhood was—in the midst of Tibetan communities all over India. We were a small family—my grandparents, parents, and my two younger brothers, one of whom passed away in 2009.

I was brought up in India, but in a Tibetan community. I grew up speaking Tibetan, but my language is slightly different from those in Tibet—Tibetans in India are poor in their own language.

Initially, I went to missionary schools—Holy Cross School in Gangtok for kindergarten, and then to St. Thomas School until Class 2. That was when my father was transferred to Delhi. The Tibetan government office was in Lodhi Road in Jorbagh and my parents lived there.

I was sent to boarding school—Tibetan Home School—in Mussoorie in Himachal Pradesh. It was established by a high-profile Tibetan related to the Dalai Lama, but it is a school under the CBSE board, affiliated with the Indian public education system. It was mainly attended by Tibetan students, although there were one or two Indian students as well. I was there until 1995, when I graduated from high school. I enjoyed school very much, but I was an average student. Math and algebra were a bit easier for me, though.

Throughout our childhood we knew that Tibet was ruled by China and that our freedom was controlled by the Chinese military government. We were told this. That is why on every tenth of March, we celebrated Uprising Day for Tibetans by marching toward the Library Chawk. There we would burn effigies of the Chinese premier and sing patriotic songs, followed by the national anthems of Tibet and India. Every student from Class 7 onward had to be present. This was and still is organized by the Tibetan government and implemented by Tibetan settlements.

When I later came to Delhi, I realized that people here do the same thing on Uprising Day. They go to Jantar Mantar in masses and protest by burning effigies and singing. Sometimes people would self-immolate as an act of sacrifice for Tibet. These days in Delhi, we are not allowed to walk to Jantar Mantar from Majnu ka Tila. We can only walk from Rajghat to Jantar Mantar. In Delhi, 90 percent of the [Tibetan] people attend the protest, but in other settlements, everybody attends.

When I grew up I wanted to be a businessman. But I never thought about whether I would work in India or Tibet. We Tibetans are not so serious in thinking about Tibet. Only 5 percent think seriously. The rest, we don't think about what we'll do in the future.

When I was in Class 10, I selected Commerce and then started to plan this as what I wanted to do. So I went to Delhi University to study for a Bachelor of Commerce.

I made Indian friends for the first time at Delhi University. Initially, they didn't know what Tibet was. They thought I was Chinese. Some asked, "In what part of India is Tibet?" Others thought I was from the northeast [of India, where people also have Mongolian features]. But I think that, except for the color of my skin and how I speak, there is no difference between myself and an Indian. I was born in India. I am an Indian by birth. I have birth rights here. I have Indian citizenship and an Indian passport. Most Tibetans are not Indian citizens here, but they have residential certificates. Tibetans are not really 100 percent refugees.

We run a travel agency. I am in charge of tours within India—booking travel and hotels for tours to Jaipur, Dharamsala, etc. Our customers are from Europe, the USA, and Australia. We have an online presence and get customers through recommendations.

I never thought of setting up for life in Tibet. I want to visit, of course, but I have two countries—India and Tibet. If Tibet becomes free, I would definitely go. But I would keep one leg in each country. Tibet is my fatherland and motherland. But I was born in India. I want to make my life in both places.

Right now we are demanding a free Tibet, but that is not possible. The Dalai Lama wants autonomy now. That is also okay. We can enjoy the Chinese economy. We wish to have a full, free Tibet, but that is not possible. Even the Dalai Lama sees that.

I have aspirations to go to a Western country and settle there. But I think that is a dream that many other Indians have, too. It is not because India is a horrible place to live; it is just that now that I am married with three children I want to ensure a better, safer future for my children. India is the only home I know. I have been here all my life. I was born here. My family is here. I regard myself as both Indian and Tibetan. Now I am a citizen of India; we pay taxes here. I will go to Tibet if it becomes free.

Anuradha Chenoy

Second-generation "refugee" from West Punjab
Age: undisclosed (middle-aged)
New Delhi, India
January 29, 2013

Both my parents were from the other side. My mother was from Lyallpur and my father from Pindi. I'm more familiar with stories of my mother's family because my father died when I was very young.

My grandfather was a lawyer and my mother had five brothers and one sister. She was the second oldest. Her sister was married before Partition and one brother worked in Uttar Pradesh. My mother was a B.Sc. student [an undergraduate] in Lahore and luckily she completed her degree before Partition took place.

The stories that the whole family always tells are about the nation, about how they were attached to the ideas of Gandhi, their great hero, but simultaneously they would talk about the two communities living separately—the Muslims living separately. The discourse that I heard in my family was always that the individual Muslim neighbors they knew were good people and they trusted them, but as a community, the Muslims were dangerous. My relatives always felt that the individuals—their friends and neighbors—were exceptions. The story I heard was, "We gave our keys to the neighbors and left."

There were all these contradictions as well; on the one hand they revered Gandhi, but I don't think they practiced, in terms of inter-community relations, what he was arguing for. But they liked his concept of the nation, of anticolonialism. They also knew the importance of secularism. I was always relieved that my family did not support the right-wing Hindus. However, over the years I realized that despite being outwardly progressive, they harbored prejudices against "others."

My mother did not speak much about Partition. I recall that my father was very fond of Urdu poetry and the culture around it. But he, too, rarely spoke of the past—maybe because he was a busy executive. In any case, I do not remember him being negative about the past. Perhaps it is because they had the protection of the nation that they didn't feel the need to look back and tell stories. They wanted their children to grow up in this new nation and see it as their own. So unlike, say, internally displaced people who have grievances and have lost their lands for dams—now that I work and meet with internally displaced people like those in the *Narmada Bachao* [Save Narmada] movement, who are angry with the state and hence very vocal—my relatives were not angry with the Indian state. They saw displacement as a process of Partition.

Two of my mother's brothers went missing and the family used to listen to the radio every night to find out where they were. It used to be announced every night—so and so is here; so and so has been found. That's how the family found the brothers.

What is very clear is how fathers and brothers made the women promise they would protect themselves. That made it easier for the men to pack up and go. I've heard stories of women who married men who had protected them or helped them to save themselves during those terrible days. Very often these marriages took place, breaking caste barriers, but not class barriers. So caste barriers were crossed by the Punjabis well before the rest [of India] because they had to make autonomous choices by force. So, while my mother's elder sister had an arranged marriage, everyone else, including my mother, made their own choices in marrying people they met in the camps, etc. Life in the camps was tough, as the fathers had to go to government offices to make claims to get some compensation for what they had lost. Families had to live in overcrowded shelters. Girls had to fend for themselves.

My grandfather was too shattered to restart his practice, however. He left behind clients of many years' standing and did not know how to start again. He had a lot of land in West Punjab for which he was not compensated adequately; the land for land provision was very uneven. One son got one small plot in Nizamuddin [in Delhi]. They collectively got agricultural land in Haryana [near Delhi]. Now it's worth something, but the family sold it to educate themselves.

After my mother came here, she worked in the refugee camp where they lived temporarily, until her brothers got jobs, and then the family rented a house. She went on to do a Master's in social work at Delhi University as well as a B.Ed. and started to teach at a school. It was a big thing for a woman from a feudal family. She met my father at the camp and he had already started doing his Master's in social work and human resources, following which he went to the London School of Economics [in the United Kingdom]. On completing his studies, he landed a good job. These were the kind of success stories that people used to point to and say, "Look, they were refugees but they did well." It was my grandfather's insistence on education that resulted in a family of very successful, well-to-do professionals. But this was after years of great hardship.

I was twelve years old when my father died of a virus. Somehow it became untreatable, and no antibiotics at the time helped. My mother restarted her life again with three young daughters—I was the eldest. Children can feel displaced through any loss—it does not have to be Partition. That is when I understood the notion of displacement, as we had to move again.

We moved to my mother's sister's house in Lajpat Nagar [in Delhi], a very BJP-dominated area. We had no home, nothing. My mother started teaching at Springdales School, and my younger sisters and I all studied there. I had an uncle—my mother's elder brother Prem Sethi—who was very religious and a wonderful person. He never married; he was a kind of *Arya Samaji*.[5] He had a government job as a scientist, but he would help anyone, especially women, in distress. He helped women, all of whom he called *didi* [elder sister], through very difficult times, including us. He influenced us greatly, as his concept of religion was tolerant, just, and not opposed to any other.

My mother rarely spoke about my father after he died. She was so tough-ened by this whole experience of Partition that, after that, she could face the world alone. This was true for many women. The experience made women strong and resilient. But rape was another thing altogether. If that happened to anyone, they couldn't reconcile with that. They could reconcile with the loss of their land, with restarting lives, with getting married on their own without dowries, but they couldn't reconcile themselves with rape. An aunt was raped and her family disowned her, in the sense that they got her married to someone much below their class and they didn't recognize the child that was born out of the rape.

In terms of acclimatization, I think class determined experiences a lot. There were many Punjabis who became communal and a base for the BJP while ours did not. Experiences varied from family to family—there was no stereotyped model. Personally, I had a progressive instinct. I remember I was repelled by a pro-Hindu, anti-South Indian Shiv Sena rally that I saw in

Mumbai. I thought that India was a plural society—I was learning Marathi, being Punjabi, having come from a family displaced from West Punjab. Instinctively, the right wing made me shudder from when I was about seven or eight years old.

Basically, I had a very, very tough life. And it's not easy to put it into words. All I can say is that I made my personal struggle easier because I linked it with others who were even worse off, people who were displaced and could not get an education. Worse were the patriarchal and communal entrenchments. We also felt it at every stage—a widow with three girls from West Punjab was seen negatively in the 1960s, but somehow I fought it instinctively because of my uncle, as I mentioned. So for me his religion and my politics had a convergence.

Actually, I was relieved that I had to fend for myself as opposed to other girls (including all my cousins) I knew in school and college, who had stable families and who were thus married off before they knew how to say "no" to their parents.

Finally, when I went to Jawaharlal Nehru University, I met Kamal, my husband. He supported all of us—my sisters and me—as he was from a very affluent and eminent family. My mother has stayed with us always. My youngest sister, Medha Malik Kudaisya, teaches at the National University in Singapore. My other sister did her MBA and now runs a craft trust. My mother is very happy now, at eighty-six. She reads all the books and articles we write, but her views somehow remain more or less the same. I am often impatient of all these Punjabi relatives who are not able to understand the criticality of secularism. But I also have to tolerate them because of their experiences.

Munir Ahmed

Afghan refugee born in Pakistan
Twenty-three years old
Kabul, Afghanistan
January 7, 2013

My family has experienced the refugee life for more than thirty years. I am twenty-three and the eldest child of my parents. I was not born in my homeland. I have a job here in Kabul, but my family is still in Pakistan. My parents have gone through very difficult times, so I am going to tell you my story and what I have heard from them.

I have four sisters and a brother. My brother and three sisters are at school, and my sister is a *madrassah*[6] student. I attended the Naseem Lodin Primary School, which was for Afghan refugees, funded by an Afghan businessman under the Naseem Lodin Foundation. We had a very good time at the school. It was a mud house with no doors or windows. We had ten teachers; seven of them were brothers who were living at the school. It was very far from our homes.

But we felt like outsiders; we did not have our homes, our lifestyle was different from the locals'—we were obviously poorer. Our parents used to tell stories of their life before and during the war—stories about their own home and lands and about the early days of the war, their fears, how and when someone was killed, and so on.

The Russians started bombarding our villages and, at the same time, the jihadists—local warlords—started to carry out unjust assassinations. My relatives and parents left our village, spending months in other villages in Afghanistan near the border which were a bit safer. As the situation became more dangerous, they gradually started to leave for Pakistan. Not everyone could go at the same time because we were not going through official channels. The borders were blocked and the alternative routes were long and difficult to access on foot.

They found out about convoys that, for a price, could take them across to Pakistan. The convoys would take one or two members from each family and cross the border through different ways. My parents had nothing, just the stuff they could carry in their hands. They were not officially received—they did not go through immigration or any process to determine refugee status. But there were camps arranged by the jihad leaders in Peshawar—some of my relatives joined the camps, while others started to live in villages by themselves. They were not treated too badly, because our jihad leaders were fully supported by the government of Pakistan.

My parents were among those who lived in a village in Peshawar. It wasn't difficult to fit in because, like us, the villagers were Pashtun. That is where I was born and raised and educated. I grew up with stories of my homeland, of its beauty and its people. The locals in Peshawar were not nice to us, but we had our pride. We were not dependent on anyone for anything; we managed to sustain ourselves through small jobs.

My siblings and I wished to see our country during our childhood, after realizing that we had our own home, village, and relatives. I went for the first time with my grandfather. I was twelve. It was one of the best moments of my life. I was awestruck when I saw our land and our village—some houses had partially or fully collapsed, but it was still beautiful.

My parents go to Afghanistan occasionally, despite not having any desire to do so, because the situation is uncertain and they are settled in Pakistan. I do regret growing up in Pakistan and not Afghanistan, but we had only one option— to live in Pakistan. I have achieved a Bachelor of Commerce there. But I could have done that in Afghanistan, too. There were better possibilities in Afghanistan, but I could not go because I was with my family and I could not afford it.

Now there are two kinds of Afghan refugees living in Pakistan. One, those who own their own businesses, houses and have a better life; two, those middle-class people who live a good life with a low income and cannot afford to live in Afghanistan, like us. Both would prefer to live in Pakistan because basic provisions like healthcare, education, food etc., are not scarce. For your information, every day thousands of Afghans travel to Pakistan for better healthcare due to the lack of good, economical care in Afghanistan. If these facilities become commonplace in Afghanistan, refugees will automatically return. Now security and peace are an issue in both Pakistan and Afghanistan; people are not safe because the political situation is so critical and uncertain in both countries. We can live in peace when the war ends. NATO started the war to bring peace, but wars cannot be ended by wars.

Today I am an accountant and have moved to Kabul, my homeland, but my parents continue to live in Peshawar. I want to have a good job to better support my family and to live in Afghanistan. They have lost everything in Afghanistan, but they are thinking about going back now for two reasons. The first is that the situation in Pakistan is also uncertain these days; the second is that I have a job here, so we can afford to live in Afghanistan. I don't want to live as a refugee anymore.

Farooq Dawood Herekar

Second-generation Muhajir
Fifty-three years old
Karachi, Pakistan
October 13, 2012

I was born in Sawantwadi, 750 kilometers south of Mumbai. I grew up in Karachi. I studied from Class I to Class I2 at St. Patrick High School and College. I enjoyed sports more than academic subjects.

In our case, migration from India to Pakistan was by choice rather than having been forced. My father studied in intermediate[7] and medicine in Mumbai. On becoming a doctor, he joined the Indian Army in the Medical Corps in 1944. I was born in Sawantwadi in December 1947, right after Partition. Soon after Partition, a choice was given to the Indian officers: either remain in the Indian Army or join the Pakistan Army through migration. My father, without hesitation, opted for Pakistan, without taking any relatives into his confidence. He sacrificed his property rights, friends, and relatives, and came to Pakistan. My mother, her sister, and her husband, who was in the Indian Navy as a civilian, followed my father to Karachi in Pakistan. I was only one year old at that time. My father was transferred from the Pakistan Army to the Pakistan Navy, where he served for twenty-two years. The Navy provided accommodation, security, and medical care. The Pakistan Navy was a big family in itself. All of my father's colleagues were from the Armed Forces and therefore there was no problem at all. I was too small to know about the fate of other migrants.

At the time of Partition, all of my father's relatives were in Mumbai and Sawantwadi and had no reason to migrate; Mumbai was a cosmopolitan city and in Sawantwadi Muslims were safe. But that was also difficult; being in the Armed Forces, the only challenge that my family faced that I can think of was of being away from their near and dear. However, my contact with my relatives in India—forty families compared to five or six in Pakistan—is still very strong. It has only been a fortnight since my wife and I visited them.

My father migrated purely for love of Pakistan. We were lucky that the people in the Armed Forces did not make us feel different for being Muhajirs. I have one son who is a commander in the Navy; his wife is also an officer in the Navy. My two daughters are doctors and another son is studying for his MBA. All of us are very patriotic Pakistanis—so much so that both my daughters refused proposals from abroad, as they wanted to remain in Pakistan after marriage. They are happily married in Karachi. I retired as a captain in the Navy after serving for twenty-eight years and never felt that I was being discrimated against as a Muhajir.

Are there Muhajirs who feel differently? Yes. You see, there are two types of migrants: one forced and the other by choice. The former bear the scars of being uprooted, relatives being murdered, the loss of property, etc. Their second generation, unlike mine, has been brought up with those stories and therefore their reactions toward India, understandably, differ from mine.

I live by President Kennedy's philosophy: "Ask not what your country can do for you, ask what you can do for your country." What I try to do is not to run any traffic signals, not to drop litter on the roads, not to use plastic bags while shopping, not to bribe anyone; if a mistake has been made, I pay the fine. These little things are being followed by my entire family. If these are adopted by others, some change for the good will come, Inshallah.

Aalo Mukherjee

Second-generation Bangali refugee
Fifty-nine years old
Kalindi, West Bengal
December 15, 2012

My father, Dr. Bharendranath Chakrabarti, was born in 1919 in Faridpur, East Bengal, which is now Bangladesh. He was the youngest of eight brothers and four sisters and they lived in Madaripur. My grandfather was the headmaster of Khaila Government High School, but he was also a landowner. The family lived in a *zamindar bari* with a huge estate.

But my father and uncles were patriots—they actively participated in the *swadeshi* [self-rule] movement and were even jailed for their anti-British activism. Then *danga* [riots] broke out and they had to leave.

They had to leave because after Partition people no longer respected them—everyone would come into the house uninvited, the boatmen wouldn't start the boat when asked. *Issa hoile saroom* [I'll start when I feel like it], they would say. It wasn't outright violence, but an atmosphere of *ottyachar* [oppression] compelled them to leave.

So it was in March of 1948, about a year after Partition, that my father, mother, grandmother, and elder brother and sister—I hadn't yet been born—

left *desh*[8] on a train and became refugees for life. Their neighbors and friends were with them as well.

They could take very little along with them, and upon arriving in Kolkata, they fell into poverty. Nevertheless, my father made it through medical school and became a doctor. In Kolkata, they spent some years in Amar Street, and then in Manik Tala which was where I was born. I grew up with stories of my parents' real *desh*.

They had lots of regrets. Strong regrets. It was their own *desh*, their real *desh*, My father would say, "I was a citizen there. It was my own land, my own home, my own family." Day after day, I saw my father cry. He would tell stories and cry. He lived with a lot of sadness. He never let go of his *Faridpuri*[9] Bangla. He spoke just like I speak Bangla now, not the "proper Bangla" spoken in West Bengal.

The government gave refugees land which was later registered in their names. There were colonies too—Jadavpur Colony, Sharad Colony, Matilal Colony, Bapujinagar Colony. These were refugee colonies, but my mother didn't like them—although her brothers took up residence there—and so we never lived in them.

In 1955 my father built a home in Birati, an area which was Muslim-dominated before Partition. My schooling mostly took place there. It was a sparsely populated area, but the people were all from *desh*—all refugees. Because of our similar backgrounds, we became very good friends, almost like family.

I was a first-year BA student in 1971 when I got married. It was only after marriage that I realized the difference between a Ghoti[10] and a Bangali. During my student years in Birati, I wasn't aware of the difference in social entitlements. After I got married I moved to Kolkata and I began to realize. When in 1979 we moved to Kalindi I became fully aware. For the first time I realized that humans are different. Even in troubled times, people may not come to your assistance. In the flat opposite mine lived a family whom I treated like my own. But they never treated me well. They were Ghotis, I was a Bangali, and it seemed that it meant that I was a lesser being. There are many differences between Ghotis and Bangalis. Ghotis still claim West Bengal to be theirs only; they still treat us like foreigners, like refugees. They are selfish, self-centered.

Bangalis, by contrast, are *dil-doriya* [loving], easy-going, with the ability to bring people closer; they are beautiful inside and out. If you come to my house at 2 p.m., you will have to have lunch with us because it is lunchtime. If you go to a Ghoti house, you won't get any food. They would rarely eat with you. We Bangalis do not harbor such sentiments. To us, everyone is equal. Not in their eyes. We never knew such things growing up. We could never imagine such things.

The only people I have seen who are beyond such dogma are *rickshaw wallahs* [rickshaw pullers] and petty shopowners. They are the real, wonderful people here who do not make such Ghoti-Bangal distinctions. They are the ones I like. They may not have money, but they are rich in their hearts because they have found *Ishwar* [God].

Kakila

Tamil refugee from Sri Lanka
Thirty-one years old
Bangalore, India
December 31, 2012

I left Sri Lanka when I was eight years old. My memories of Sri Lanka are of helicopters hovering above as we made our way to and from school. I was the eldest, with two brothers and a sister, and so I had to make sure that they were safe. My mother had trained us how to lie down flat on the street with our arms above our heads in the event of bombings. Amid this fear of bombings we went about our lives, until one day in 1990 we heard rumors of air strikes that would destroy the entire area. As the frenzy intensified during the course of the day, my parents and some of our neighbors decided to make that fateful trip to India by boat.

We hired a boatman who would take us across under the cover of darkness. It was a small boat with no roof. There were eight families—around twenty-five people—crammed into the small space. Soon after we started out, the boat began to fill up with water. Throughout the night, people took turns to bail out the water. It was a frightful journey, wrought with danger and uncertainty. We clutched each other, willing the night to be over. It was early dawn when we reached land.

The rumors had not been rumors after all. The day after we left, the entire area was flattened, leaving no visible signs of human existence.

We went to the refugee camp in Rameshwaram. We were given a room with a tin shed. We found out that most parents worried about the safety of their daughters there—they would marry off ten-year-old girls to ward off evil male attention and protect them from predators. There were such social problems, but at least we didn't have to fear for our lives.

Perhaps it was my safety that propelled my parents to send me off to a boarding school for Sri Lankan refugee children two years later, in 1992. That event changed my life. It was difficult to leave my parents in the camps, but in retrospect that was the best thing to happen to me. I got a good education, while my parents were relocated from one refugee camp to another. It was after going there that I realized how inadequate the refugee schools in the camps were. After graduation, I stayed with my parents at their camp for a while, but returned to the school with a job as a coordinator. Today I am self-sufficient and self-reliant, but my parents still live in the camp.

Over the past twenty years, the camps have improved. There is clean water now. The government has allowed refugees to build structures within their designated spaces; my parents built a bathroom. The camp residents have become like family members. Still, I think we all harbor the desire to go back to Sri Lanka. That is our home. We owned fields there, we employed forty people to help with rice and chili production, and we owned our own house.

We can go back, but we don't know what awaits us there. If we go, we will lose our refugee status here, and we will be unable to return. I have made a life for myself here, but my parents are still in limbo; they have spent their entire adult lives in a refugee camp.

Notes

1 Literally translated, *gondogol* means chaos or trouble. In this context it refers to the Pakistani military crackdown in Dhaka and elsewhere which started Bangladesh's War of Indpendence.
2 Literally, *dal-khichuri* is a rice dish made with equal parts of rice and lentils. Here, she means she is the child of an inter-ethnic couple and hence a "mixed breed."
3 Literally, *chokher bali* means "the sand in one's eyes." It is a phrase used to mean "the hated ones." In this context, they were so despised that their presence was like sand in the grandfather's eyes.
4 Literally, "lawless country" or "land of the Moghs" (Rakhine people). Used colloquially, it simply means lawless lands.
5 Arya Samaj was a movement to reform Hinduism that included, among other things, an emphasis on meditation using Vedic mantras as opposed to idol-worshipping, giving non-Brahmins access to education and language (especially Sanskrit), and celibacy. This movement was founded by Swami Dayananda in the late 1800s. His followers are often called Arya Samaji.
6 An Islamic bording school, usually affiliated with a mosque.
7 "Intermediate" denotes high school graduation. It is part of the verbiage left over from colonial times where "matriculation" was the final examination taken at the end of Grade 10 and "intermediate" was the final examination taken at the end of Grade 12. The names of the exams have since changed in India, Bangladesh, and Pakistan (as well as in England!), but they are still used colloquially.
8 *Desh* means "country" or "nation," but depending on the context, it could mean "homeland" or simply "home."
9 Faridpur-style. Faridpur is a district in Bangladesh.
10 Colloquially, people who are "originally" from West Bengal are Ghoti, as opposed to the Bangalis, who came to West Bengal after Partition. As such, there is rivalry between the two groups in terms of who the "real Bangalis" are.

3 Contentious politics and refugee protests

Are refugees voiceless? Citizens may make demands on their states, but refugees are not citizens; they are often rendered stateless. Refugees who have obtained work, legally or otherwise, are unable to use the tool to which workers often resort in order to demand change—namely the withholding of labor power. Going on strike is most likely to ensure that they never get another job. If undocumented Latino/Latina immigrants stopped work for a day, California would no doubt come to a standstill; South Asian refugees, like refugees almost everywhere, have no recourse to this most potent "weapon of the weak" (Scott 1985). Refugee groups are thus vulnerable to all kinds of exploitation but have little bargaining power; the ways in which they can express their grievances are limited. Yet, there are examples of refugee groups protesting about poor living conditions in India and Bangladesh; in doing so they are in fact making demands, either upon the state or on international organizations. The Chin refugees, for instance, around 5,000 of whom live in Delhi, regularly use the Jantar Mantar[1]—a favored site for political rallies and demonstrations—for protests. Thus, they try to draw the attention of the Indian government to the squalid conditions in which they live and the harassment and discrimination they face, whether in Delhi or in Mizoram.

"Refugees inside the official camps have some voice and our support encourages that. There has been and still are several instances of protests, sometimes against mistreatment by government officials, sometimes against UNHCR officers," said an aid worker in the Rohingya camps in Bangladesh. "But they are usually suppressed."

"Entrepreneurs" and "organic leaders"

Among refugee groups there is the potential for "organic leaders" to come forward who are in charge of refugee welfare and can mobilize refugees to engage in protest activities. These leaders, invariably camp dwellers themselves (where there are camps) or else community leaders (among the Tibetans in Delhi, for example), play multiple roles under the influence of numerous, often contradictory, forces. While these organic leaders might mitigate protest activities because they want to be perceived as being willing to make compromises, if unappeased they may use their position to incite agitation. In turn, if the leaders do not appease aid workers and government officers (such as "camps in charge"[2]), refugees risk negative consequences. For better or worse, therefore, camp leaders are important in recruiting and mobilizing people for demonstrations, to the extent that they are successful in effecting change at some level. Securing public services and amenities can help to boost the status of the leaders and enhance their mobilizing capacity.

For instance, most Bihari refugees in the Geneva Camp in Dhaka want to be repatriated to Pakistan, but they rarely make that demand because they have realized that the government of Bangladesh is incapable of effecting repatriation. The decision would have to come from Pakistan. Thus, when the refugees were offered Bangladeshi citizenship in late 2008, most accepted, although many continue to live in the camps. The camps continue to be led by their *netas* (leaders), whom they elect every few years. The *neta*'s role is to liaise with the mayor's office, negotiating rations and other entitlements. *Netas* also help to provide public services, if only to win re-election. Abdur Rahman, a *neta* in 2008, started an informal school in his camp and negotiated with the government of Bangladesh on behalf of the camp dwellers at a time when UNHCR was not involved in their protection.

The Chin refugee population in Delhi also has an organization for welfare services called the Chin Refugee Committee. The president of the organization, Bo Nai, describes it as an organization that aims to address and solve the problems that Chin refugees face in Delhi. Its officers are elected from among the refugee population and their collective task is to present their problems to NGOs and international organizations, primarily UNHCR. As India does not support the refugees financially or otherwise, they organize fundraising events and also rely on donations from the refugees themselves. The money is used to provide assistance with hospital bills and interpretation, given that most Chin refugees speak neither Hindi nor English. It is also used to facilitate capacity building and the establishment of workshops on human rights, refugee rights, women's rights, and so on. The primary role, however, is to develop contacts with international organizations and to put forward demands in a collective manner. The Rohingya refugees in Bangladesh have committees as well—the Block Management Committee and the Camp Management Committee—to which refugees are nominated in order to help to run daily affairs in the camps and blocks in which they live.

Similarly, the Tibetans have the Tibetan Resettlement Office and the Resident Welfare Office, both of which serve to provide welfare services to Tibetans. The Tibetans receive more support from the Indian government than the Chin do, which is why they have a two-tier welfare system. The Tibetan Resettlement Office is a bureaucracy under the Tibetan government-in-exile, and the Resident Welfare Office is a local organization funded by the Indian government, although its officers are elected from among the Tibetan refugee population or diaspora. These two bodies coordinate with each other to implement policies and uphold the interests of the refugee group. They also organize protests and movements on specific days. There is a loudspeaker system in the Tibetan Refugee Colony that is used to disseminate such information: "The PA system is used for major announcements such as meetings and demonstrations at Jantar Mantar," said a Tibetan nurse who works at the clinic provided by the Tibetan government-in-exile.

The emergence of leaders from among the refugees would seem to corroborate the literature on "contentious politics," more specifically on resource mobilization and organization, which presents strong leadership as a precursor to successful protest (Meyer and Tarrow 1999; Giugni et al. 1999; Meyer 2007). As Tarrow states,

> Leaders invent, adapt and combine various forms of collective action to stimulate support from people who might otherwise stay home. Albert Hirschman had something like this in mind when he complained that Olson regarded collective action only as a cost—when to many it is a benefit. For people whose lives are mired in drudgery and desperation, the offer of an exciting, risky and possibly beneficial campaign of collective action may be a gain. Leaders offer forms of collective action that are inherited or rare, habitual or unfamiliar, solitary or part of concerted campaigns. They link them to themes that are either inscribed in the culture or invented on the spot, or—more commonly—blend elements of convention with new frames of meaning.
>
> (1994: 20)

Protest leaders are thus "entrepreneurs" who opportunistically exploit conditions (often of suffering) and who mobilize for protests because this is the least costly option. As Tarrow (2011: 8) articulates, "Organizers exploit political opportunities, respond to threats, create collective identities, and bring people together to mobilize them against more powerful opponents." This does not discount his earlier argument that social movements become possible only when such organizers/leaders can "tap more deep-rooted feelings of solidarity or identity" (ibid. 1994: 6).

Certainly, it isn't difficult for protest leaders to mobilize at short notice, given the compact geography of their camps and communities. Protest leaders in camps do not have to invest heavily in the recruitment process because encamped refugees are the targeted recruits. In domestic politics, it is a truism that political rallies and protests—at least those led by the major political parties—are often bought and paid for, with hundreds bused in for the price of a free lunch. Among refugee populations, incentive structures need not be highly developed or include money—if camp dwellers can be convinced that protesting will improve their plight, they are likely to participate. In fact, if the protest leaders are able to frame their demands in a manner that convinces refugees that the outcomes will be beneficial, refugees may be willing to pay for mobilizations as well, provided they believe that change is possible.

"If conditions are poor, we voice our concerns. We protest. When Médecins Sans Frontières withdrew from the camp, we protested. Unfortunately, a few people died then. We were not able to get them back, but the Ministry of Health set up a clinic in the camp. Compared to MSF, the MOH is a bureaucratic nightmare, but it's something," said a Rohingya camp dweller in Kutapulang Camp in Cox's Bazar.

However, refugee leaders are propelled by their communities, which tend to be more politicized than local communities by virtue of their experience of fleeing conflict. Leaders might thus be *born of* protests and protest movements. Even those with a limited background in protest activities will nevertheless find it necessary not only to communicate refugees' demands to the appropriate authorities and negotiate the services they get, but also to show that they are acting in the interests of the refugee community or camp by mobilizing for protests when all else fails. The Geneva Camp Biharis have thus periodically engaged in nonviolent protests, in the manner of Gandhi's *satyagraha*. During the mid-1980s one such protest led to riots and is remembered as a negative experience that led to many arrests and gave the camp a bad reputation. Since then, say the camp dwellers, they have not engaged in riots—only peaceful protests and processions. As one of them put it, "These processions help our leader to tell the government what we need in the camps."

Citizens and refugees

Leadership and recruitment alone do not account for the emergence of protest movements. Even if there are leaders, there are risks to engaging in protests, for both individuals and groups. Tarrow informs us that

> [t]he base of all social movements, protests, rebellions, riots, strike waves, and revolutions is *contentious collective action*. Collective action can take many forms—brief or sustained, institutionalized or disruptive, humdrum or dramatic. Most of it occurs routinely within institutions, on the part of constituted groups acting in the name of goals that would hardly raise an eyebrow. Collective action becomes contentious when it is used by people who lack regular access to representative institutions, who act in the name of new or unaccepted claims, and who behave in ways that fundamentally challenge others or authorities. Contentious collective action serves as the basis of social movements ... because it is the main and often the only recourse that most ordinary people possess to demonstrate their claims against better-equipped opponents of powerful states. This does not mean that movements do nothing else but contend: they build organizations, elaborate ideologies, and socialize and mobilize constituencies, and their members engage in self-development and the construction of collective identities.

(2011: 8)

However, local authorities have greater coercive license and exercise less caution when it comes to refugee populations (as we see in the case of the Rohingya in Bangladesh, for example). Individual refugees and refugee groups risk further marginalization or even deportation if they engage in protests. Individuals and families can enjoy the benefits accrued through protest undertaken by others, while collective action might result in collective punishment.

What, then, explains why protests happen? Lipsky (1968), Gurr (1970), Kitschelt (1986), Tarrow (1994, 2011), and Fearon and Laitin (2003) all suggest that grievances form the basis of protest movements, but that it is "political opportunities" that help to explain the "when" and "why" of social movements. Political opportunities are defined as

> consistent—but not necessarily formal; permanent or national—dimensions of the political environment which either encourage or discourage people from using collective action. The concept of political opportunity emphasizes resources external to the group—unlike money or power—that can be taken advantage of even by weak or disorganized challengers. Social movements form when ordinary citizens, sometimes encouraged by leaders, respond to changes in opportunities that lower the costs of collective action, reveal potential allies and show where elites and authorities are vulnerable.
>
> (Tarrow 1994: 19)

Similarly, Skocpol (1979) argues that the military weakness of the state, aggravated by external shocks, brings about political instability and change; North and Weingast (1989) argue that state weakness (in the administrative sense) creates incentives for people to revolt and demand change when they are seriously suppressed. Kalyvas (2006) argues that the weakness of the state (or of the insurgents) brings about political instability, but in this analysis, unlike those of Skocpol and of North and Weingast, it often has no bearing upon structural change.

It becomes clear that this discussion about political opportunities cannot be used when conceptualizing why refugees protest; the state apparatus, relative to the refugee groups, will always be stronger. Even when political opportunities (as defined by Tarrow) arise, refugees and their leaders will be unable to take advantage of them. The stability or weakness of a state, moreover, have little to do with whether refugees are willing to mobilize for protests, because their demands and their numbers make them very different from minority national groups vying for political power. Hannah Arendt once observed that refugees lack the right to have rights. This underscores the limitation of the framework of contentious politics, for it remains focused on *citizens'* protests, and however marginalized they may be, citizens actually can claim to have rights. For this reason, refugees are arguably the weakest political group in a society—if not in terms of cohesion, then in terms of voice.

Yet, as James Scott (1985) and scholars of subaltern studies remind us, the subaltern or subordinate classes can engage in forms of resistance even when power asymmetries make collective action difficult, as is certainly the case with refugees.

> Most forms of this struggle stop well short of outright collective defiance. Here I have in mind the ordinary weapons of relatively powerless groups: foot dragging, dissimulation, desertion, false compliance, pilfering, feigned ignorance, slander, arson, sabotage, and so on. ... They require little or no coordination or planning; they make use of implicit understandings and informal networks; they often represent a form of individual self-help; they typically avoid any direct, symbolic confrontation with authority.
>
> (ibid.: xvi)

However, refugees also engage in overt protests and mobilization in addition to covert "everyday forms of resistance." In order to explain protests among refugees, two observations are useful. First, mobilization among refugees in South Asia is facilitated by the fact that refugees are encamped, often for years, which renders them a captive audience and allows for quick information dissemination. The lack of adequate services, moreover, is generally shared by all. These factors allow for the coordination required to make collective action possible. For example, the Bihari camp in Dhaka lacks proper toilet facilities. The odor that engulfs the camp is evidence enough of the problem. That impacts all camp dwellers, which in turn serves as a unifying factor. Second, this unified voice often has an audience with some capacity to address and redress their grievances: co-ethnics and international aid organizations.[3] When there are shared grievances and leaders among the refugees, these allies are often the link between refugees and the state, serving to close the information gap. Refugees thus protest when they know that these allies can take up their cause and make demands on the state on their behalf.

International organizations not only create opportunities for protest; they are also often the service providers, who can redress grievances. International organizations thus have several roles: (1) they can publicize protests which can help to garner more support and resources; (2) they can effectively legitimize protest activities; (3) they themselves can be allies and help to pressurize host authorities to address grievances; and (4) they can directly address some of the grievances. State authorities value their relationships with international organizations because they legitimize the government's position in the international community and also serve to share the burden of harboring refugees. Organizations such as UNHCR are not only credible bodies that can provide the goods or services that refugees want, but also allies in pressurizing the state to address some grievances, such as state repression that aid organizations cannot control.

There are challenges, however. As a camp dweller in the Rohingya Kutapalang Camp in Cox's Bazar put it, the government officers—camps in charge in this case—are the "lords." They can make the refugees' lives very comfortable, but they can also make them miserable. Apparently, international organizations and NGOs have to watch what they say and do in order to be able to work in the camps. Even if NGOs advocate on behalf of the refugees, their communication with government officers has to be amicable so as not to antagonize them and thereby create an unwelcome outcome. "When we protest, we need to be careful of what language we use because otherwise it may be counterproductive," explained the camp resident.

Shared ethnicity and the existence of co-ethnics in the state also serve to create opportunities for protests. If refugees are able to gain the sympathy of co-ethnics, then they can pressurize the government and international organizations to improve refugee conditions. Protests, then, serve the purpose of garnering sympathizers from among the local population. Since governments are usually more responsive to the demands of their citizens than to those of refugees, co-ethnics in the receiving country can be a useful ally. It is not surprising, then, that "empowered refugees" are those who have co-ethnics in the state—the Tamil and Bangali refugees in India, for example, enjoy a certain degree of freedom and even rights that other refugee groups in the region generally do not.

Protests are useful because they appeal to these sympathetic outsiders—co-ethnics, locals, international organizations, and human rights organizations—who can pressurize the host into actions such as improving living conditions. Protests, hence, aim to arouse the sympathy of those who can influence policies. As the goodwill of locals, human rights organizations, and international organizations is important to the authorities, they are in a position to pressurize the authorities to actually address the refugees' grievances. So, protests can be explained by (1) grievances indicated by poor conditions and host hostility; and (2) opportunities to use protest for influence, indicated by the presence of international organizations and co-ethnics in the receiving country. International organizations such as UNHCR can provide double benefits because they can pressurize the host state into reforming policies in addition to providing direct benefits to refugees. Thus, only when we redefine "political opportunities" as opportunities for developing a relationship with the state—in this case through international organizations and co-ethnics—without probing state weaknesses can we use social movement verbiage to discuss protests among refugees.

Grievances: internal or external?

That protests have their origin in grievances is obvious enough. Where refugees are concerned, their status as non-citizens means not only that their appeals often lack a sympathetic audience, but also that their grievances are specific and contingent. Having fled conflict and sought refuge in another land, refugees face political repression and police violence, have no prospect of immediate return, and face poor living conditions and the animosity of locals.

Repression is one factor that can incite protests: while low and high levels of repression can tame protests, mid-level repressive tactics serve to antagonize people.[4] Hibbs (1973), who provides one of the first systematic empirical analyses of the causes of collective protest, argues that traditionally the tendency in the literature has been to assume that repression has a deterrent effect, which is not often the case. He shows that violence is not pervasive in the societies considered to be the most permissive or repressive, but in those with "middle-sized" capabilities. It is in the moderate societies that the regime's coercive power is sufficient to antagonize certain groups but not enough to suppress opposition (Poe and Tate 1994; Goldstone and Tilly 2001). In terms of the effects of actual acts of repression, the short-term or immediate response to repression is usually more violence, but in the long term repression has a deterrent effect (Hibbs 1973; Rasler 1996). Yet, in the face of repression, protesters may also substitute violence with nonviolent forms of protest (Lichbach 1987). Repressive states can expect a certain level of reprisal as a response to state aggression. Even low levels of repressive tactics can foment anti-state sentiments, thus exacerbating grievances, although excessive repression can create a situation of suppression.

Why do host states turn hostile? They face a dilemma when welcoming refugees: they want to provide relief, but at the same time, they do not want the refugees to stay forever. The longer they stay, the greater the burden. Initially, irrespective of the expected length of stay, the host government is unlikely to repress refugees owing to scrutiny by international actors such as UNHCR during that period. However, following the initial phase, if the host government expects the refugees to stay for a long period of time, it is likely to use repressive tactics to induce them to leave, as in the case of Lebanese policy toward Palestinian refugees.

States use repressive tactics more frequently on stateless people than on persecuted refugees because the expected length of stay for the former is usually much longer (according to the report on "Worst Places for Refugees" [USCRI 2009a]). This can be illustrated by the experience of refugees in Thailand: the Thai authorities treat Karen refugees with greater civility than that accorded to the Rohingya, who are stateless. However, if the receiving state fails to recognize refugees drawn primarily from stateless populations as stateless and takes no measures to redirect them within a reasonable time frame, it may produce a path-dependent situation in which it is less costly to host refugees than to use force to move them. Such was the case with the Bihari population living in Bangladesh in 2008: Bangladesh eventually had to grant citizenship to its Bihari refugees because it was unable to find an alternative resolution whereby India or Pakistan would take them back. The crucial element is the expectation a state forms during the initial period of refugee inflows. Although the state may not be in a position to act at that time, the expectation it forms will have repercussions on its policies and whether they incite protests.

Poor living conditions may form a basis for grievances as well (Lischer 2003; Baron et al. 2003). Such conditions reflect the resource capability of the host and its international support; if such conditions persist for a long time, they can become one of the "shared concerns" that the literature shows can incite protests. Poorer countries, owing to their limited resources, cannot provide a high standard of living for their own citizens, let alone for refugees. In addition, if there are no international organizations supporting the host with refugee protection or ensuring a minimum standard of support, there is little chance that conditions will improve.

A longer expected stay can also induce protests directly; when refugees themselves realize their predicament, they may find protest activities to be the only way to make their voices heard. Until a framework is set up to channel demands and address them, an extension in the expected stay can increase protests.

Much of the limited literature on rebels in refugee camps assumes that protests are geared toward the sending country (Adelman 1998; Zolberg et al. 1989) and often have little to do with the politics of the states in which they find refuge, although there are some claims that large camp sizes, a high number of males, and poor living conditions can create violent situations in refugee camps (Loescher 2001; Cambers 1982; Jacobsen 1996). This creates confusion as to what counts as "protests" and how to label greater degrees of political participation and violent activities.

Empirically, many of the world's refugee situations involve rebels who are hostile to the regime in the sending country and who harbor separatist sentiments, whether in terms of demanding regime change, regional autonomy, or even an independent state. In India, for example, the Tamil refugees from Sri Lanka demand regional autonomy, while the Tibetan refugees have demands ranging from self-determination to ending repression. However, such political interests are unlikely to be served well by mere protests, because the host state has no control over such factors. Thus, the claim that I make is that *protests among refugees are a function of state-based sources of grievances such as living conditions, but the desire to protest is realized when there are opportunities in the form of the support of international organizations and co-ethnics.*

Empirical analysis

In analyzing my claim, I examine two questions: (1) What kinds of grievances lead to protests, internal or external? (2) Do opportunities—the existence of international organizations and co-ethnics—give rise to protests?

To answer these questions I use "protest" as the dependent variable. Protests are peaceful demonstrations generally geared toward making demands. The Rohingya in Bangladesh, for example, often mobilize in order to demand working rights and the ability to move away from the camp grounds. "Protest" here is a categorical variable that takes on 0 when there are no protest activities in refugee camps and 1 when protests in the form of demonstrations or riots occur in camps. Protest leaders are the natural leaders who emerge from elections at committee level. The recruited protesters are refugees who hold grievances and want to change the status quo, but do not have access to arms and weapons. Given the categorical nature of the dependent variable, I use an ordinary logistic model to assess the predicted probability of protest activities.

Independent variables

The independent variables used for each type of protest are provided below.

"Internal grievance" variables

These are variables that foster grievances among refugees and form the basis of protests.

State hostility: State hostility or aggression (used interchangeably) is when the host initiates the use of force by means of attacking refugees in camps. This is a categorical variable which takes on the value of 1 when the host country uses force against refugees and 0 otherwise. Although hostility can foster grievances, the expectation is that it will lower the probability of protests, especially since protesters do not have retaliatory capability. State hostility is the variable that is potentially endogenous.

GDP per capita: GDP per capita is used to proxy the host's ability to protect refugees (in terms of providing a security force in the camps) and also its ability to provide a good standard of living. A lower GDP per capita prevents the state from adequately providing even basic services, which can imbue refugees with a sense of discontent, leading them to protest. A rich state not only is able to provide welfare services and safety, but can also provide jobs, precluding the need to protest. It is difficult to assess exactly how GDP per capita impacts protests, but we can look at it as a "general" measure of host capabilities.

Poor living conditions: Poor living conditions can provide the basis for grievances among refugees that make them susceptible to recruitment for protest activities. Such conditions can serve to unite refugees to demand better protection collectively, thus increasing the probability of protests (see Figure 3.1). Poor living conditions is a crude measure based on population density and sanitation facilities. For example, in 2003 the Bihari Camp in Dhaka had 273 toilets (with open roofs) for 79,000 people. This qualifies as poor living conditions.

"External grievance" variables

The variables used here to analyze non-state factors that contribute to refugees' grievances are as follows.

Expected length of stay: The expected length of stay is measured by assessing the media's presentation of how long a particular refugee group will remain in the camps each year (see Figure 3.2). This is determined by (1) the

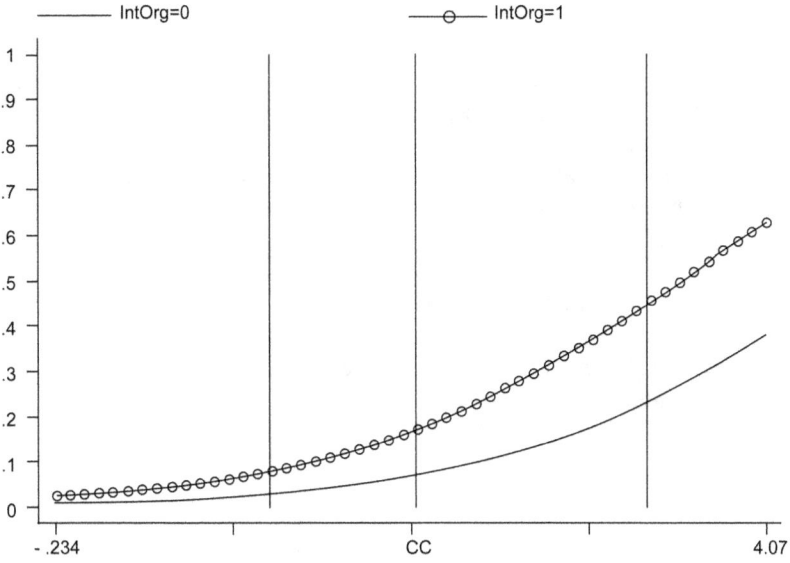

Figure 3.1 The effect of the presence of international organizations on protests for varying covariate contribution

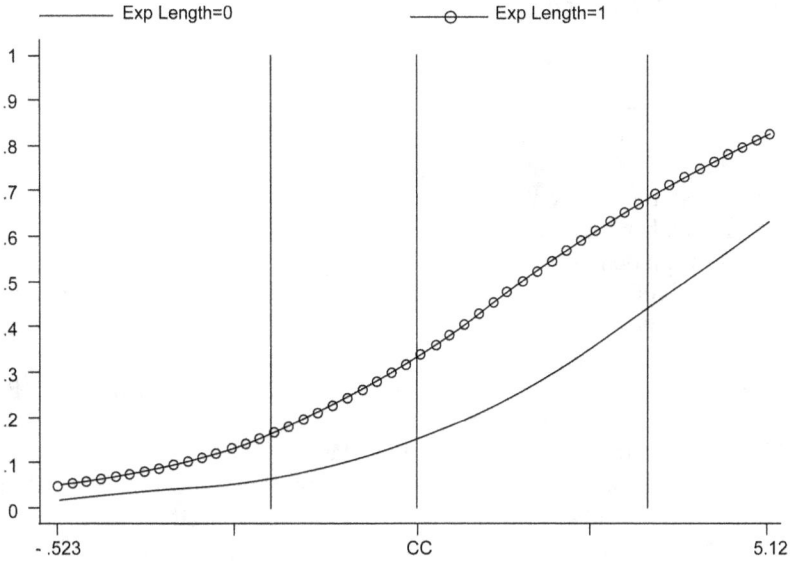

Figure 3.2 The effect of the expected length of stay on protests for varying covariate contribution

situation in the sending country, which will make return easy or difficult; and (2) talks between relevant actors regarding repatriation. A long expected stay can be a source of frustration for both the host and the refugees who have fled their homes "temporarily." It may make intuitive sense to say that refugees in protracted situations are more prone to protest, but in such circumstances they are also aware that protesting will not resolve the crisis; in fact, protesting may be the excuse that the host state uses to repress refugees. The variable takes on the value of 1 if the expected stay is long, 0 otherwise.

Relationship between the receiving and sending countries (alliance): The host state's relationship with the sending country can bind it in several ways. If the receiving state has a hostile relationship with the government of the sending country, for example, the host is likely to be more sympathetic toward the refugees' cause. In the simplest terms, a receiving state can be pro- or anti-sending country, which will in turn determine the host's behavior toward refugees from that country:

- Pro-sending country: This type of host, in showing support to the sending country, is likely to be antagonistic toward refugee groups. It may even repress the refugees in a show of support to their country of origin, as in the case of Macedonia showing its support of Serbia in 1998 by opening fire on Albanian refugees escaping Kosovo.
- Anti-sending country: This type of host, all other things being equal, will welcome refugees and even highlight their plight in order to make a statement about the (perceived) sending country's domestic turmoil.

The variable "alliance" takes on a value of 1 if the host is pro-sending country or neutral and 0 if the host is anti-sending country.

Separatist: Whether the refugee group is separatist by nature is used to gauge the relationship between refugees and the sending country. The variable indicates whether the particular refugee group in the host country is a separatist group demanding self-determination or sovereignty (coded 1 if so, 0 otherwise). If refugee groups are interested in regional autonomy or another uniting cause, they are generally more cohesive, with strong ideological bonds. For example, the refugees who traveled to India from East Pakistan were members of the Mukti Bahini[5] by default, and the idea of a liberated Bangladesh was a force that cohered refugees, despite poor living conditions. The likelihood of the groups to engage in anti-host activities is low because (1) the host is giving them refuge; and (2) the group is more focused on its own nationalistic (or otherwise) goals; to engage the host is time wasted. Thus, in this case I would not expect separatist tendencies to have a positive impact on protests.

Rate of refugee inflow: A higher rate of inflow indicates that more people are available to partake in protest activities. The variable counts the number of new refugees in a given year. This variable serves two purposes. First, it signifies the entry of new refugees, and hence new recruits for engaging in protests. Second, new refugees may be prone to protesting because they are unhappy in their new surroundings and demand better conditions (assuming that if they wait, their demands will never be met). If the latter is the case, then including "poor living conditions" as a variable should counter its impact. At the same time, new refugees may be too scared or too relieved to have escaped violence to be motivated to engage in protests.

"Opportunity" variables

These variables are those that allow protests to develop because an "opportunity" has arisen to resolve or address refugees' grievances.

Presence of international organizations: This is a categorical variable indicating whether or not at least one international organization is involved in the protection of refugees in any given country in any given year for a particular refugee group (see Figure 3.3). As identified earlier, international organizations not only provide direct benefits to refugees (and hosts), but also can put pressure on the host to address grievances. Thus, the presence of international organizations can be seen as "opportunities" for protests.

Shared ethnicity: This variable is coded as 1 when refugees share an ethnic identity with at least one ethnic group (majority or minority) in the host country and as 0 otherwise.

Shared ethnicity with groups within the host country is likely to have a positive impact on protest behavior for two reasons: first, the local groups serve as a support base that legitimizes protests, and second, as identified earlier, co-ethnics are potential sympathizers who can pressurize the

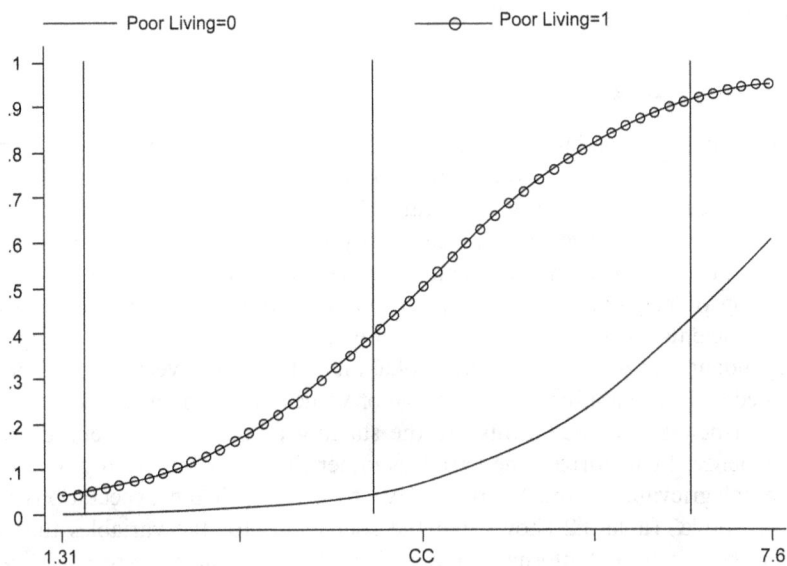

Figure 3.3 The effect of poor living conditions on protests for varying covariate contribution

government to bring about change. Part of the reason that the government of India could not ignore the plight of refugees was the shared Bangali identity among Bangladeshis and West Bengal residents.

Preliminary findings

An examination of the cross-tabulations in Table 3.1 shows that of all refugee groups that live in poor conditions, one-third (33.33 percent) are involved in protest activities (thirty-nine out of 105 cases). This may not be very informative because of all cases where conditions were good, the percentage of protests was slightly less (30.77 percent). However, there were only thirty-nine cases in total where living conditions were good. This indicates that poor living conditions can lead to a greater incidence of protest, although the difference is minor.

Of all the cases where the host was hostile, only 10 percent of the cases involved protest activity, whereas when the host was not hostile, 37 percent of the cases involved protests. This indicates a dampening effect, because when the host is hostile, there are fewer cases of protests than cases of no protests.

Table 3.1 also shows that given the presence of international organizations, 51.06 percent of cases involved protests, while in their absence only 23 percent involved protests, indicating that their presence is associated with more protests. Where there were co-ethnics in the host country, 67 percent of the cases involved protests, while when there was no shared ethnicity, only 16.82 percent of the cases involved protests. Thus, both in terms of the presence of international organizations and shared ethnicity, we obtain preliminary support for the "opportunity" explanation.[6]

Regression results

Table 3.2 provides the findings of the logistic regression that shows how "internal grievance," "external grievance," and "opportunity" impact protests. A coefficient is deemed statistically significant if the p-value is less than or equal to 0.05 (otherwise the level of significance is provided). The signs on the coefficients indicate how the independent variables affect the probability of protest, positively or negatively. As the logistic model is nonlinear and probabilistic, the coefficients alone do not tell the entire story. In order to see how a given independent variable impacts the probability of protest, we need to look at the predicted probabilities for the range of values of the independent variable.

Nevertheless, the coefficients are the starting point for interpretation. For convenience, I categorized the variables under the labels "internal grievance," "external grievance," and "opportunity" to align with the expectations presented above. Table 3.2 shows that the coefficients for the variables that fall under the labels of "internal grievance" and "opportunity" are statistically significant, while none of the "external grievance" variables are. This provides support for the hypothesis presented here: protests are likely when there are

Table 3.1 Cross-tabulations

Grievance variables			

Poor living conditions *Protests*	0	1	*Total*
0	27 (69.23%)	70 (66.67%)	97 (67.36%)
1	12 (30.77%)	35 (33.33%)	47 (32.64%)
Total	39 (100%)	105 (100%)	144 (100%)

State aggression *Protests*	0	1	*Total*
0	60 (61.86%)	44 (81.48%)	104 (68.87%)
1	37 (38.14%)	10 (18.52%)	47 (31.13%)
Total	97 (100%)	54 (100%)	151 (100%)

Opportunity variables Shared ethnicity *Protests*	0	1	*Total*
0	89 (83.18%)	14 (32.56%)	103 (68.67%)
1	18 (16.82%)	29 (67.44%)	47 (31.33%)
Total	107 (100%)	43 (100%)	150 (100%)

International organizations *Protests*	0	1	*Total*
0	81 (77.88%)	23 (48.94%)	104 (68.87%)
1	23 (22.12%)	24 (51.06%)	47 (31.13%)
Total	104 (100%)	47 (100%)	151 (100%)

grievances based on state-related factors and when opportunities arise in the form of sympathetic allies who can make demands on behalf of refugees from the state. Let us examine the table in more detail.

"Internal grievance"

The variables relevant to examining the "internal grievance" claim are GDP per capita, poor living conditions, and state hostility. The coefficient for GDP

Table 3.2 Logistic regression for protests

Protests	Coefficient
Internal grievance variables	
GDP per capita	1.33e-13***
	(3.65e-14)
Poor living conditions	2.91***
	(0.99)
State hostility	−2.185***
	(0.687)
External grievance variables	
Expected length of stay	0.762
	(0.915)
Alliance	−0.436
	(0.963)
Separatist	−0.704
	(0.7722)
Rate of inflow	1.159
	(0.904)
Opportunity variables	
Shared ethnicity	3.09***
	(1.162)
Presence of international organizations	1.87***
	(0.66)

***$p < 0.01$, **$p < 0.05$, * $p < 0.1$
Standard errors are given in parentheses
Number of observations = 149
Log likelihood = −41.284164

per capita is positive and statistically significant at all reasonable levels of significance, countering the notion that poor host countries breed animosity among refugees because they are unable to provide the basic necessities. Instead, it can indicate that in wealthier states, refugees are more demanding, perhaps because the state has the resources to meet those demands. However, the coefficient is almost 0, indicating that the host country's income level actually has a very small impact on refugees' proclivity toward protests. This is an important finding in the South Asian context, where states often claim that refugees are in fact "illegal immigrants" seeking better opportunities in the receiving state. The almost-zero impact provides preliminary evidence to show that the wealth criterion has little impact on protests or on the demands that refugees make; refugees are not using a pretext to avail themselves of better services. It may be relevant to note, nevertheless, that all three receiving countries are developing countries, as are the countries of origin of most refugees there. Therefore, apart from large-scale violence, the economic conditions they face may not be very different, which can perhaps explain the near-zero coefficient.

Poor living conditions, arguably the main variable that can be the basis of grievances, increase the probability of protest activities as shown by the positive, statistically significant coefficient for the variable. It comes as no surprise that poor living conditions engender grievances among refugees that make them naturally prone to protests, but it counters the assertion made in the previous paragraph about refugees' tendency to tolerate harsh conditions because of their plight. In the South Asian context, these are not contradictory. While refugees' proclivity toward protests is not determined by how wealthy the state is, the camp environment is a different entity, especially because most of the refugee crises in the region are protracted ones. People may not protest if they think that their predicament is temporary, but if they realize that in the near term the camp will be their home, living conditions begin to matter to the extent that refugees are willing to protest about them. Thus, protest leaders can use living conditions as a unifying factor to mobilize protests successfully.

Unsurprisingly, state hostility/aggression has a statistically significant negative impact on protests. Figure 3.4 visualizes its impact and shows that, for varying covariate contribution, the difference between state aggression and nonaggression increases, then decreases. The concept of covariate contribution (cc) literally means the contribution of all the noninteraction term covariates to the model, to isolate the impact of the interacting variables. When dealing with helpless protesters who have no access to weapons, repressive tactics thwart protests simply because these refugees do not have the capability to fight back. Why do such state actions not result in a strong resolve among refugees to fight back? There may be several reasons. First, protesting in the face of state aggression may result in harsh punishment, even deportation. Second, refugees who flee violence have a high level of tolerance for violence. Third, host aggression may signal to refugees that protesting will not change their circumstances—a more lethal form of protest may be necessary in order to counter the aggression. Whatever explanation we find most convincing, we see that host aggression can successfully suppress protests. For example, the Rohingya in Bangladesh are routinely under attack by Bangladeshi authorities, yet they rarely engage in protests. However, it is worth asking

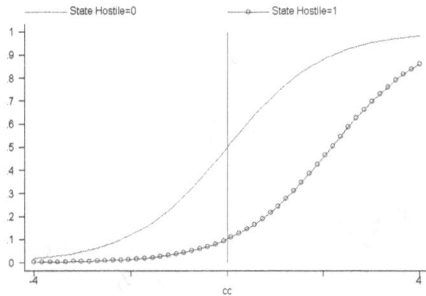

Figure 3.4 The effect of state hostility on protests for varying covariate contribution

whether state aggression was responsible for the rise of the Rohingya's para-military force, the Rohingya Solidarity Organization (RSO), in Bangladesh.

Summarizing the "internal grievance" explanations, then, we see that poor living conditions forms the basis of grievances. The more general measure of host capabilities—GDP per capita—has a very small impact on protests, while state aggression dampens them. However, when it does not lead to protests, host state aggression can still foster grievances and can ultimately induce militarization.

"External grievances" explanation

In terms of the external sources of protests, one can see that none of the variables are statistically significant at any reasonable level. "Alliance" has a nega-tive impact on protests; i.e., formal agreements or friendship between the host and sending countries lower the probability of protests. This may be because refugees are aware of the friendship and the preconceived negative attitudes that the host may have, and hence the refugees refrain from protesting out of fear of repression. This finding is not statistically significant, however.

The negative coefficient for "separatist" shows that the existence of separatist groups does not increase the probability of protests. Although such groups may have ambitious plans to bring about political change, their mode of expression is unlikely to be through protest activities. Such groups may well have unsuccessfully tried protesting in their home countries as a way to demand reforms. Thus, protests are likely to be deemed useless. Such groups are likely to be more inclined toward militarization than protests, which I discuss further in Chapter 4.

A higher inflow rate indicates that more people are available to engage in protest activities. New refugees are also easy targets for recruitment, owing to the fact that they are new and often need help from their compatriots to settle down in their new environment. New refugees require little convincing to join protest activities because they have been politicized recently, which makes them passionate about bringing about change. Although the coefficient is positive, supporting such notions, it is not statistically significant at any reasonable level.

The coefficient for "expected stay" is positive as well, which means that if refugees think they will remain in the receiving state for a long time, they are more likely to engage in protests. When both refugees and locals realize that refugees will be in the host country for a long time, refugees, aware of their predicament, feel the need to make their demands known before they get into a path-dependent outcome whereby they are left with few rights. They protest while they still have some media attention, before the state becomes too complacent to ensure a minimum level of services. The coefficient, in this case too, is not statistically significant. This may be because of the prevalence of long-staying refugees in the three countries; the protracted nature of most cases does not generate incentives to protest.

Thus, none of the "external grievance" variables can explain protests among refugees in camps.

"Opportunity" hypothesis

This brings us to our redefined opportunity hypothesis about the role of allies in prompting protests among refugees. Table 3.2 shows that both the presence of international organizations and that of co-ethnics have a positive, statistically significant coefficient, indicating that these variables indeed increase the probability of protests. Figure 3.3 demonstrates that when international organizations are present, the probability of protests is higher relative to absence, given covariate contribution. As discussed earlier, international organizations and co-ethnics provide the "opportunity" for which protest leaders are waiting.

The presence of international organizations signals the existence of a framework to fulfill the demands that refugees make. Protests develop because protest leaders know that protesting can yield a positive outcome in terms of addressing their demands. International organizations can appease refugees in the long run by providing the required necessities, so that refugees no longer need to protest in order to receive benefits. In the short term, however, protests among refugees may develop to communicate demands to international organizations and to get them to become allies who can pressurize the authorities to address grievances.

As discussed earlier, shared ethnicity provides refugee groups with a support system that can be sufficiently empowering to compel them to engage in protests. In acknowledging this support, protest leaders may become bolder when demanding services for refugees. More importantly, groups of co-ethnics can also pressurize the relevant authorities to address grievances. Their role can be more crucial than that of international organizations, because co-ethnics are unlikely to have any agenda beyond sympathy and camaraderie and are hence less susceptible to suspicion.

Thus, the regression results provide evidence to support the notion that grievances alone are insufficient—protests become likely when international organizations and co-ethnics support refugees as allies. Based on the findings, then, one can make the argument that poor living conditions provide the basis for grievances among refugees. When international organizations and co-ethnics are present, it provides protest leaders with the opportunity to communicate demands in the only way that they feel is effective: through protest activities, by capitalizing on the grievances of refugees in order to unify them as a group and mobilize protest.

Theoretically, the findings imply that the weak do engage in protests, not merely in covert, everyday forms of resistance; refugees with "no rights," too, demonstrate for access to better welfare services. However, they do so only when influential potential allies with *legal*, and therefore legitimate, rights exist to communicate their demands to service providers. In a perfect world, every citizen should be a potential ally, but as the findings show, some pre-existing mode of cohesion and solidarity, namely the existence of co-ethnics and international organizations, allows refugees to voice their demands in the form of protests.

Concluding remarks

This chapter shows that protests by refugees are not very different from protests by citizens, despite refugees' political weakness, because they are able to utilize allies within the state system to put forward their demands. Thus, refugees cannot be deemed to be helpless victims without agency. Given grievances and opportunities, they too can demand better welfare. The fact that refugees are encamped together, often for years, means that much of their experience is shared. This engenders a sense of camaraderie and makes collective action possible.

The main state-related factors influencing protests appear to be, first, how safe refugees are in camps; second, whether refugees are "protected"; and third, whether they enjoy a minimum standard of living—all factors that the state and/or international organizations can ensure. It is coincidental that in trying to address protests, this chapter ends with notions of refugee protection, much like the majority of studies on refugees. Although these findings are limited to the subcontinent, one might make the case—as many already do—that the demand for refugee protection is more universal.

Notes

1 Jantar Mantar is an open museum that houses thirteen giant architectural astronomical instruments including a sun clock built during the Mughal era. Today, the space in front of the museum is a popular protest site.
2 "Camp in charge" is the official term used for government-appointed camp supervisors and administrators who are "in charge" of the running of camps.
3 Although refugees have an ally in the form of the working classes and the poor in the host country, they are easily scapegoated for raising labor supply and hence dampening unskilled workers' wages in many instances; this in turn makes them unwanted in the eyes of locals.
4 High-level repressive tactics create a situation of suppression, thereby mitigating protests, whereas low-level tactics are not severe enough to incite antagonism.
5 Mukti Bahini, or Liberation Army. This army was formed spontaneously by Bangali armed personnel, paramilitary forces, and civilians following (West) Pakistan's military crackdown in East Pakistan on March 26, 1971.
6 The bivariate relationships help us to see how many cases we are dealing with in each category. One of the boxes (the case where there are no protests and the camp conditions are good) contains only twelve cases. This indicates the need for a larger dataset.

4 Camp militarization for state interests

"Honesty is the best image."

(Poster, Customs Office, Patparganj, Delhi)

In Chapter 3 we saw that refugees are not voiceless victims without agency. In fact, they engage in protests and exercise their voice, even though state structures serve to marginalize them. In this chapter I respond to the second stereotype that refugees face: that they are insurgents, even terrorists. As Loescher and Milner argue,

> Long-term refugee populations are a critical element in ongoing conflict and instability, obstruct peace processes and undermine attempts at economic development. Recurring refugee flows are a source of international conflict: they generate instability in neighboring countries and trigger interventions by host states and regional actors, and refugee camps can serve as bases and sanctuaries for armed groups that are sources of insurgency, resistance and terrorist movements.
>
> (2005: 8)

Much of the literature describes pro-liberation forces in refugee camps in negative terms: as militants, insurgents, warriors, refugee warriors, warmongers, and so on (Adelman 1998; Lischer 2003; Lischer 2005; Leenders 2009; Loescher and Monahan 1989). Through these lenses, concerns arise because of the negative impact refugees can have on the receiving country: they may create instability in camp areas in terms of disrupting economic activity and the existing social fabric; they can create a climate of insecurity and criminality and instill fears that violence will escalate among locals. As Loescher and Milner explain,

> The direct threats faced by the host-state, posed by the spillover of conflict and the presence of 'refugee warriors', are by far the strongest link between refugees and conflict. Here, there are no intervening variables between forced migration and violence as the migrants themselves are actively engaged in armed campaigns often, but not exclusively, against

the country of origin. Such campaigns have the potential of regionalising the conflict and dragging the host-state into what was previously an intrastate conflict.

(2005: 31)

In this fashion, the scholarship tends to highlight the contagion of conflict and the spread of civil war. As Salehyan and Gleditsch surmise,

Refugee flows from Liberia contributed to instability most prominently in Sierra Leone, but also in Guinea and Cote d'Ivoire; forced migration led to conflict in several Balkan states; and refugees from Rwanda were involved in conflicts in the Democratic Republic of the Congo.

(2006: 338)

According to this line of argument, conflict spreads because refugees can often be rebels. Zolberg et al. (1989: 275) coined the term "refugee warriors" to discuss rebel groups that are "highly conscious refugee communities with a political leadership structure and armed sections engaged in warfare for a political objective, be it to recapture the homeland, change the regime, or secure a separate state." Similarly, Adelman (1998: 4) depicts rebels as "refugee warriors if they have fled their homeland and live in neighboring states, most often in refugee communities, and launch attacks against the regime in power in their homeland from bases in the neighboring states." He argues that the emergence of refugee warriors can be explained

by how regional states and the international system treated these refugee warriors; in other words, refugee warriors are not so much a product of "root causes" but of failures—sometimes deliberate—in the management of conflicts and, more specifically, the management of the plight of the refugees themselves, whatever the original causes.

(ibid.)

Adelman also posits "preconditions" for refugee warriors:

The preconditions of being a member of a refugee warrior community are: first, the person is a refugee in the sense that the person, or that person's parents or even grandparents ... fled the geographical territory of a homeland; second, that person uses violent means aimed at overthrowing the regime in power; third, the base for waging the violent conflict is normally located in refugee communities in a neighboring state; and, fourth, the refugees are not fighting on behalf of their host state as surrogates of that state.

(ibid.: 2)

While the first three conditions are straightforward enough, the fourth warrants more attention, because states often support militarization covertly. As Stedman and Tanner (2003: 8) point out, "in today's world, many host governments are either complicit in the political and military manipulation of the refugees (as in Pakistan, Thailand, or Zaire) or lack the capacity to protect them (as in Lebanon)." Adelman is aware, however, of the multilevel forces that produce the refugee warrior:

> Refugee warriors evolve into quasi-independent armed forces with national interests of their own and are not merely, or even primarily, the surrogates of the states who finance and arm them. Refugee warriors also result from the failure of the international community either to take any effective action in finding a permanent solution to the refugee problem, or from stemming the ability of the refugees to take up arms and resort to violence to solve their problems. Refugee warriors are more a product of international political and military relations, as well as the misuse of humanitarian aid, than the internal conflicts or the legitimacy crisis which produced the refugees in the first place.
>
> (1998: 4)

Furthermore, the literature posits that militant groups "manipulate refugees" for militant purposes, in order to gain both human and material resources by pilfering humanitarian aid (Adelman 1998; Terry 2002; Lischer 2005; Stedman and Tanner 2003). In addition, as Salehyan (2008) argues, refugee camps provide excellent bases for militant groups, which often choose to organize transnationally in order to oppose state repression, and make it more difficult for states to monitor and prevent their activities.

In order to gain support among refugees, these warriors exploit the nature of the conflict that the refugees fled (Lischer 2005). Manipulation is easy if refugees have been driven from their homeland deliberately (i.e., targeted for ethnic, religious, racial, linguistic, or other reasons) and continue to feel under attack. In addition, if refugees are "majority defined," i.e., they believe that their "opposition to events is shared by the majority of their compatriots," they are more likely to become rebels than those who believe that they form a minority group even within their ethnic group and thereby do not receive any kind of support from their community (Kunz 1981: 44).

There are many who argue that the very existence of refugee camps is founded on humanitarian aid; refugee camps act not only as centers of aid distribution, but as externally imposed "safe zones" and fertile targets for recruitment (Bakewell 2001; Adelman 1998). Humanitarian aid performs the obvious function of adding resources to a war economy that can be controlled and directed by militant groups, thus consolidating their power, control, and legitimacy in the region (Terry 2002; Stedman and Tanner 2003). Militants can also acquire resources through "taxing" refugees after they receive their stipends from aid organizations. As Lischer (2003: 84) explains, "It is not uncommon for refugee leaders to levy a war tax on the refugee population, commandeering a portion of all rations and salaries."

Thus, the narrative can be summed up as follows. Refugees are responsible for the spread of conflict from one country to another because some are "refugee warriors" who coerce refugees to take part in militancy and pilfer aid in order to sustain militarization. Viewed in this light, refugee warriors are very similar to war entrepreneurs, as depicted in the literature on the subject of civil wars, with greed a motivating feature of militarization (Collier 1999; Fearon and Laitin 2003). In this chapter I outline the South Asian case to argue that, at least in this context, militarization cannot be regarded as terroristic.

In 1971 ten million refugees trekked from Bangladesh to seek refuge in India; they craved a separate state of their own and during their stay contributed to the liberation war at home in whatever capacity they could, including establishing training camps. I posit that these refugees/rebels had a legitimate claim to demand political change in East Pakistan. While they may have been a source of insecurity in India, the fact that they fought for self-determination does not make them a terrorizing force. There are two reasons for this: first, it matters whether or not refugees procure arms and weapons to engage local authorities or fight their own war; and second, India was sufficiently strong to stop the "terror." Instead, India provided material and military support to the Mukti Bahini. Hence, when conflict "spreads," it is not merely a product of refugees' commission but the state's omission, especially in the context of South Asia.

Stedman and Tanner argue that

> militarization ... appears to be part of a larger strategy of warring parties to manipulate refugees and the entire refugee regime established for their protection. Hence some refugee camps become a breeding ground for refugee warriors: disaffected individuals, who—with the assistance of overseas diasporas, host governments, and interested states—equip themselves for battle to retrieve an idealized, mythical lost community.
>
> (2003: 3)

In examining militarization in South Asia, I take my cue from Stedman and Tanner (2003) to argue that it is only under conditions of separatist self-determination that refugees become militants, and even then they do so because the state is complicit in militarization. Armed mobilization is not only justified but supported by the state if it serves the interests of the state. The very same state labels such refugees as "insurgents" and "infiltrators"; however, this serves the purpose of uniting people on the basis of identifying the "militant other."[1]

The South Asian case

In South Asia, realist principles dictate much of regional politics amid expectations that India and China will be the next superpowers. India, the world's largest democracy and the land of 461 ethnic groups (identified in the Indian Constitution as Scheduled Tribes), worries constantly about a rising China. Not surprisingly, many of its domestic policies, even refugee policies (if the ad hoc way in which India treats refugees can be called policy), are influenced by the desire to contain China. This is not the goal of a rising power, as Mearsheimer (2003) would argue; the ultimate goal of a great power is hegemony, which entails control over other countries. Thus India, in trying to contain China's growth and in projecting its own power in the region by controlling weaker neighbors such as Pakistan, Bangladesh, Sri Lanka, Nepal, Bhutan, Myanmar—often by manipulating the refugees they produce—acts in a very realist fashion as it vies to be the regional hegemon in South Asia.

The situation is not so straightforward, however. At the height of the Cold War, India's prime minister, Jawaharlal Nehru, was one of the key figures of the Non-Aligned Movement (NAM), which stood against the domination of superpower blocs while supporting international cooperation as a means of resolving international disputes. India still purports to uphold norms of cooperation and humanitarianism in its foreign policy. In balancing its realist interests (in the form of regional hegemony) with its desire to uphold its image as a benevolent international actor, India finds itself manipulating refugees to serve both purposes.

Domestically, militarization has allowed India to (1) sustain anti-refugee sentiment by identifying refugees (such as illegal Bangladeshis and Sri Lankan Tamils) as a threat to national security, thereby fostering national unity; (2) justify its refusal to sign international treaties (such as the Treaty on the Non-Proliferation of Nuclear Weapons); and (3) blame domestic problems on refugees, from unemployment to the limited provision of welfare services (especially in the northeast, which borders Bangladesh and Myanmar). Internationally, India has been able, first, to keep in check and control the politics of refugee-sending countries by arming refugees (Sri Lankan Tamils, Bangladeshis), which allows India to maintain "peaceful ties" without appearing aggressive; second, to maintain the appearance of a liberal foreign policy when in fact its motives are realist (as demonstrated by its many "issues" with neighboring "small states," such as those involving water-sharing, the demarcation of enclaves, the exchange of prisoners, and unfair trade practices); and third, to project power indirectly by using refugees as weapons and undermining the sovereignty of neighboring countries (such as in Kashmir). In concrete terms, India can "balance" the influence of China and Pakistan not only through nuclear proliferation but by supporting separatist elements which can potentially "divide" a country and thus threaten the survival of such a state.

In Pakistan, the calculations are somewhat different. While Pakistan is not in a position to vie for superpower status, it has been a transit spot for superpowers for decades now. Although in terms of state positions Pakistan is squarely behind the United States in its "war on terror," it covertly supports the refugees because the Afghans in Pakistan have public support for reasons of ethnicity and religion. This is a good example of the difference between de jure and de facto law. During the Soviet occupation of Afghanistan, Pakistan's support of militancy brought material gains from its US ally. At present, Pakistan continues to enjoy material support from the United States while turning a blind eye to militancy. Part of the reason why Pakistan is forced to look away is that the interests of Islamists and anti-imperialists there coincide. In an era of US-sponsored drone strikes that kill civilians on a regular basis, it is difficult for the newly elected democratic Pakistani government to tell its citizens that they should support imperialism. At the same time, even if the Pakistani government wanted to expel Afghan refugees, for example, it could not, because (1) co-religionists in Pakistan and the Pakistani Taliban support the Afghans; (2) Pakistan received a considerable amount of aid during the 1980s and after 2001 to provide refuge to Afghans and to support the US "war on terror"; and (3) Pakistan would face international rebuke for expelling refugees. Undeniably, Pakistan's patronage of Afghan refugees, for whatever reasons, has allowed militants to become operative.

Relative to India and Pakistan, refugee camps in Bangladesh have been less militarized. Only in recent years has the RSO emerged with the aim of armed struggle. However, the Rohingya population in Bangladesh is divided over the issue of armed struggle, which is why militarization is episodic. On the host state side, ignoring militarization serves the purpose of appeasing the sending country, especially if the sending country has patrons. At a time when Myanmar has patronage from China and North Korea, neither Bangladesh nor indeed India would wish to antagonize the Myanmarese military junta by overtly supporting militarization. However, both countries hope that permitting militarization to continue can bring about political change in Myanmar, as a democratic Myanmar is in the interest of both India and Bangladesh. Covert support of militarization among the different Myanmarese ethnic groups enables India and Bangladesh to maintain strong ties with the Myanmar government while at the same time allowing the forces of change to operate within their territories.

While Bangladesh is not remotely close to being a great power relative to India, the two countries share a strong record of democratic governance and autonomy in formulating national and foreign policies, unlike Pakistan, where policy-making has often been subject to foreign imposition. This becomes an important element in the context of militarization, because militarization among Afghan refugees in Pakistan has been a function of the United States' role in Pakistani politics. Consequently, refugee policies in India and Bangladesh are a product of state preferences and propaganda, unlike in Pakistan, where the state tries to balance *real* and *imposed* preferences. Thus, in India and Bangladesh, the politics of militarization highlights the contradictory nature of state preferences. Neither wants rebel groups from other countries to come and bring their wars with them. At the same time, the state rhetoric "supports" the oppressed, anti-imperial movements, and self-determination. Paradoxically, when minority or refugee groups express desire for freedom, the state labels them as anti-nationalists, traitors to their states, and terrorists, much like the literature (the Indian state's labeling of Kashmiris who seek independence as terrorists is, perhaps, the best example of this). Such convoluted preferences stem from the inherent contradiction in a nationalist stance that often produces xenophobia and from the incentive to manipulate refugees to maintain unity against a socialist stance which supports minority rights and self-determination, both of which India and Bangladesh seem to think can coexist constitutionally. Part of the ad hoc-ism we see in refugee protection is a function of this contradiction.

Pakistan, in contrast, finds itself officially tied to US rhetoric. The economic dependence on US aid prevents it from overtly exercising its will, as a state as well as a representative of the people. In light of public support for the Pakistani Taliban, the state finds itself precariously balancing domestic and international politics, realizing that the two levels are neither mutually exclusive nor independent. Thus, during the Soviet occupation of Afghanistan, Pakistan provided material and military support to the *mujahideen*,[2] actively promoting militarization as a US "ally," but during the current US occupation of Afghanistan it has been unable completely to thwart militarization owing to domestic support for it.

What brings about militarization? The existence of nonmilitarized refugee camps show that militarization is not always inevitable; the political context of conflict does not mean that the camps will necessarily be militarized. The Bihari refugees in Bangladesh wanted political change, but they did not engage in militarization. The Tibetans in India are not militarized either, although that may change in the near future. The Myanmarese Chin refugees in India are not militarized. The Sri Lankan Tamil refugees in India were not militarized in their early days. What these cases indicate is that militarization is not possible unless there is patronage, overt or covert. Refugees on their own, despite politicization and separatist ideals will not have the will or the ability to militarize unless it is sanctioned. Thus, Stedman and Tanner's (2003) argument that militants manipulate refugees to engage in militancy does not apply here; if it did, then there would be more cases of militarized refugee groups in South Asia, given that most refugee groups had or have separatist incentives. Adelman's (1998) argument that rebels need separatist interests ("with national interests of their own") for militarization seems to be more apt in the South Asian context.

In the cases of refugee crises related to liberation struggles—the Bangladeshis and Sri Lankan Tamils—rebel groups imported the leadership structure and hierarchy from the refugee-sending country and used the camps as a base for separatist operations from relative safety and security across the border. During Bangladesh's War of Independence, the government-in-exile—the leaders—in India formed training camps alongside the refugee camps for military exercises. In the Sri Lankan Tamils' struggle for liberation, rebels mingled with refugees with the intention of using the refugee camps as bases.[3]

However, militarization need not be a refugee group-specific characteristic or description that is constant; camps can remain civilian for years before refugees decide to engage in militancy, which happens in protracted situations (when there is no "permanent solution to the refugee problem," as quoted above). In such cases, incentives for militarization need not be imported from the country of origin; they may stem from a sense of futility in a protracted crisis, for example. If we examine the behavior of Tibetan refugees in India, for example, we see that group leaders channeled their activities into broadcasting their demand for a free Tibet, whether in the form of nonviolent protests or self-immolation. However, now that the Dalai Lama has agreed to an autonomous state within China instead of a separate state, factions are emerging within the Tibetan camp. The Tibetan Youth Congress (TYC), in particular, is still hopeful that a free Tibet is still possible. There is also recognition among TYC members that an armed struggle may be necessary to continue this fight; since 1959 the nonviolent movement has yielded very little, according to Lobsang Dorji, the general secretary of the Regional Tibetan Youth Congress in Delhi. In Bangladesh, the RSO emerged in the 1990s as an autonomy-seeking organization that began to engage in armed struggles after years of peaceful existence in the camps. The realities the Rohingya face—a protracted situation with no definite time frame for their repatriation and continued military repression that creates fresh refugees each year—fostered an environment conducive to militarization. According to Moe Myint at the BBC Burmese Service[4], the porous border between Bangladesh and Myanmar means that the refugees are aware that the political situation in Myanmar has yet to find any resolution to the Rohingya "issue," which gives the Rohingya an incentive to militarize. The two cases, Tibetan and Rohingya, show that that militarization is not a constant for a particular group but can emerge over time. In this sense, militarization is a dynamic process that waxes and wanes.

Although most of the refugee groups in South Asia demand some form of "freedom," militarization serves them differently. While militarization resulted in the formation of a new state, Bangladesh, in other cases militarization has failed to bring about any form of political change. A closer look at the Rohingya population warrants this question: why have the Rohingya not been able to secure a (federal) state for themselves through armed struggle?[5] The answer lies in the lack of unified support for armed struggle, according to aid workers in Cox's Bazar. Arguably, it is because the Rohingya's fight is for civil rights, something that in most other cases already exists. The Rohingya have had to accept a Myanmarese constitution that renders them stateless; what they demand is a change in the constitution. At this point, many feel that an armed struggle may well undermine their cause. Hence, the difference in opinion among the "leaders" regarding the appropriate course of action has resulted in a fragmented refugee population that sometimes engages in a form of armed struggle but is predominantly focused on welfare issues in the short run.

The narrative is somewhat different for the Tibetans. The TYC's interest in militarization stemmed from the realization that there is little possibility for change; while self-immolation did inspire Hollywood movie stars like Richard

Gere to speak up on their behalf, it did not have the desired effect of a "free Tibet." That the world, in the wake of 9/11, may perceive self-immolation as equivalent to suicide bombing does not help their cause. In the meantime, the TYC has come to the realization that nonviolence as a strategy has failed. The futility of the nonviolent movement produced the desire for armed struggle, according to TYC representatives. This kind of rebel formation does not require the "infiltration of rebels" from Tibet; they are very much homegrown. Thus, the Tibetan and Rohingya cases not only highlight the dynamic nature of the emergence of rebels but also show that the utility of militarization varies across refugee groups, which in turn can challenge the leadership structure.

Why do refugees participate in militarization? Refugees support militant groups because they seek protection and security at a time when the state is unable to do so, and when international organizations cannot do much. UNHCR has only two offices in India, one in Delhi and a field office in Chennai. There are many horror stories of refugees trekking across the country to reach a UNHCR office in order to obtain identity cards. It is not surprising that refugee leaders and rebels have more clout among refugees than unreachable "authorities." This perspective is in line with Zolberg et al. (1989), who argue that refugees are sympathetic toward rebels, but counters Lischer (2005) and Adelman's (1998) assertion that refugees have "mixed feelings" about rebels.

Although there appears to be a consensus that refugees will have incentives to misappropriate foreign aid for purposes of militarization (Lischer 2003; Loescher et al. 2008; Salehyan 2008; Achvarina and Reich 2006), it is unclear whether aid promotes militarization (through leakages and pilferage) or whether it tends to flow to the worst-hit areas that have already become radicalized, thereby resulting in a spurious correlation between aid and militarization. Nevertheless, there is no evidence to suggest that aid has been pilfered directly by rebels in the three countries. The lack of evidence may be explained by the dearth of accountability and transparency that UNHCR sometimes suffers owing to the existence of multiple partner organizations, multiple levels of authority, and multiple ways in which aid is disbursed, according to a UNHCR representative in Washington, DC (interview conducted on May 16, 2008).[6] However, "indirect pilfering" does take place: because separatists have nationalistic goals, refugees who believe in the cause are often willing to sacrifice a portion of their rations in order to support it. The Bangali refugees in 1971, for example, gave up personal assets in order to contribute to the liberation effort. Thus, "taxation" in this context is a legitimate fundraising tool and not a coercive tool, as depicted in the literature.

The militarization of refugee camps in the South Asian context, then, relies on separatist movements that have state patronage. Stedman and Tanner make the case that

> [i]t is important to recognize … that host states may be either incapable or unwilling to take measures to ensure the civilian character of refugee camps. They may be incapable because they are weak states and lack the

capacity to maintain security, law, and order in refugee camps. They may be unwilling because they find militarized camps a useful foreign policy instrument for serving their national interests.

(2003: 9)

All three states—India, Bangladesh, and Pakistan—are strong enough to thwart militarization if they want to. It is not that they are "incapable," but that they are unwilling. It is no surprise, then, that the Indian military provided training to Bangladeshi freedom fighters in 1971 and to the Liberation Tigers of Tamil Eelam (LTTE, commonly known as the Tamil Tigers) in Sri Lankan camps in the 1980s. However, both the Bangalis and the Tamils had pre-existing incentives to use the camps as training grounds; militarization was not only a function of the state's agenda. Nevertheless, India's support gave rebel leaders the freedom to exercise their will.

Thus, leaders among refugees may originate in their own countries, whereby these leaders enter the receiving country as leaders already, or through the refugees' experience as refugees in interacting with their own country and the patronage rebels receive from the state. However, militarization, even when there is no official state patronage, is unlikely without state support, if not impossible. Rebels take high risks when they engage in militarization: it can lead to deportation, border closures, and the use of outright repressive tactics and force against the refugee population. Consequently, refugees and any rebels among them engage in explicit armed struggle only when they have state patronage, explicitly or implicitly. In the three cases of explicit militarization studied here—the Afghan refugees in Pakistan, the Sri Lankan refugees in India, and the Bangali refugees in India—all had state support, either overtly via the military or covertly via intelligence services. These are all cases where states encouraged militarization to serve another political goal (more on this in the next chapter). However, state support did not undermine the refugees' will in any of these cases. Instead, the overlap between the interests of the state and the refugees resulted in an outcome of state-patronized militarization.[7]

In the South Asian context, then, the following options are available to the states:

1 manipulate refugees to militarize by financing them and creating rebels
2 support existing militants and militarization through patronage and supplying arms
3 keep aware of militarization, but ignore it
4 keep aware of militarization but fail to control it

There are two further options:

5 remain unaware of militarization
6 clamp down on militarization through repressive tactics/force, and/or close down the border to prevent further influx of militants

States employ options 5 and 6 very rarely. It is only when the state apparatus is very weak that it may be unaware of militancy among refugee groups; without the state's complicity, militarization is almost always impossible. Option 5 is an ex post facto option that states draw on after they lose control over a militarization which they themselves have supported. In these situations, the use of such tactics absolves the state from any responsibility for the militarization that it supported and at the same time allows it to identify militarization as an external threat that calls for national unity.

Thus, it is states that manipulate refugees and either support militants or turn them into militants in order to serve state purposes. There may always be separatist incentives, but state patronage is ultimately what makes militarization a reality. Intentions alone are insufficient.

Empirical analysis

The claims put forward thus far are based primarily on observations across South Asian states in the context of militarization. An obvious problem with assertions made in such a fashion is that they may be selected on the dependent variable, i.e., choosing those cases of militarization where the state was complicit and then arguing that the state was a patron of militarization. In order to test whether a more general argument can be made, albeit within the South Asian context, I use a logistic model with militarization of refugee groups (in camps) as the dependent variable, which facilitates comparison between militarized and nonmilitarized refugee groups.

This section brings together the theoretical explanations for militarization and assesses whether the variables identified in fact led to militarization in India, Bangladesh, and Pakistan with special state patronage and aid. The dependent variable "militarization" is defined as weapons and arms infiltration in camps or nearby areas (yes/no coded as 1/0). The appropriate statistical model for a binary dependent variable is the logistic model corrected for panel data, which is utilized in this chapter based on the same dataset used in Chapter 3.

Data and expectations

The variables used in this study and the expectations are described as follows (see Appendix 1 for details).

State complicity: State support or complicity has been construed in a broad sense—if the state actively supports or simply *ignores* militarization that is taking place within its borders, then the state is *complicit* in militarization. The assumption here is that states are strong enough to prevent militarization if they want to; the only reason they would not actively prevent or stop militarization is when there is no will to do so. Such disregard can stem from an interest to see militarization succeed, in which case the state may even provide material support, or from an indifference toward the outcomes of militarization.

Thus disregard, or passive support, as well as active support constitutes state complicity.

Separatism: When camp militarization is aimed at the sending country, potential rebels are exogenous elements that use refugee camps and their people for the "cause." The aim of such efforts is usually to bring about political change in the country of origin no matter at what the cost; hence this type of militarization is difficult to curb. This leads to the idea that rebels who bear anti-sending country sentiments increase the probability of militarization. This has been operationalized as a dummy variable.

Aid: Aid is the amount of money allocated to a given country each year by UNHCR (in US dollars). As the discussion of aid and pilferage shows, the expectation is that aid increases the probability of militarization if separatist groups exist and if the host is hostile.

International organizations: The presence of international organizations may well be a double-edged sword. On the one hand, host governments may be more welcoming if they are "sharing the burden," but on the other hand, the presence of such organizations may also encourage camp militarization if aid is not channeled properly (which in itself is costly and hence often disregarded). The presence of international organizations in the process of protection, rehabilitation, repatriation, and resettlement also serves as a signaling tool for the various actors involved. To the host country, for example, their presence indicates that the refugee crises will be resolved within a short time frame, whether in terms of repatriation or resettlement. Some hosts may even find their presence lucrative, as it signifies inflow of foreign currency. International organizations is a dummy variable that takes on 1 if there are international organizations active in the refugee protection and repatriation process and 0 if there are none.

Alliance: Militarization becomes likely also because of host countries' strategic interests. India's support for (East) Bangalis in 1971 had much to do with ethnicity, but the strategic role it played cannot be ignored: by allowing militarization to take place, India indirectly propelled the division of Pakistan, a rival country. Such strategic interests are not rare. One way to understand or measure strategic interests is by checking whether the host and sending countries are allies or rivals. If the two are allies, the host has the incentive to temper militarization, given the capability to do so; if they are rivals, no such motivation exists. Thus, alliances lower the probability of militarization, given capabilities. I code the status quo times as 0, times when there are border disputes as 1 (bad relations), and times of state-level visits as 2 (good relations).

Ethnicity: This chapter began with Table 4.1 which identifed cases of militarization in India, Bangladesh, and Pakistan. Ethnic ties appear as a category as well; in four of the five cases where refugee groups had ethnic ties with groups within the host country, there was also militarization (Davis and Moore 1997; Saideman 2001; and Woodwell 2004 find support for this notion of transnational ethnic ties creating solidarity and hence supporting militarization). This "coincidence" by itself does not establish a causal relationship, but it does elucidate the understanding that ethnic ties and cleavages can

Table 4.1 Refugee groups and militarization in South Asia

State	Refugee origin	Status	Ethnic ties	Militarization
India				
	Sri Lanka (Tamil)	Ongoing	Yes	-
	Pakistan (Kashmir)	Ongoing	Yes	-
	Pakistan (Bangladesh)	Resolved	Yes	-
	China (Tibet)	Ongoing	No	No
	Bangladesh (indigenous)	Ongoing	No	No
Bangladesh				
	Myanmar (Rohingya)	Ongoing	No	-
	Pakistan/India (Bihari)	Resolved	No	No
Pakistan				
	Afghanistan	Ongoing	Yes	-

create incentives in the host country to promote militarization. In the data used here, the cross-tabulation between "militarization" and "shared ethnicity" shows that there are no instances where there is shared ethnicity but no militarization. Accordingly, in all instances of shared ethnicity there are militarized refugee camps. This prevents the use of the variable in the data analysis, but provides sufficient information to claim that shared ethnicity has a positive correlation with militarization in the South Asian context.[8]

Location of camps: This variable identifies whether refugee camps border the sending country. Proximity to the sending state can increase militarization because refugees fear cross-border attacks and arm themselves for defensive purposes, and because militarization provides easy access to arms and weapons from compatriots still in the sending country. However, most camps in the three countries have been in border regions; hence there is little variation in the data, preventing its use in the data analysis.

There are several limitations here. First, refugees from all bordering countries could not be included in the dataset owing to unavailable information. Excluded are the Burmese (Chin) in India, as well as the "illegal immigrants" and tribal refugees (Jammu) from Bangladesh. Second, the dataset only contains information pertaining to refugees in refugee camps (and not those outside of camps), again, for reasons of data availability. Although this was not problematic in the context of Chapter 3, where I examined protests in camps, in the context of militarization it is an issue because it is not necessarily the case that militancy occurs only in camps—it may well occur outside of camps. Consequently, militarization is underrepresented in the data.

Regression analysis

The appropriate model for the analysis of camp militarization, given the dataset, is a logistic model that is adopted for a panel data structure. The two effects that are of interest for the study are *separatism* and *complicity*. I argue that separatism is a cause for militarization, but on the other hand, I also argue that without state complicity militarization would be difficult—if not impossible—for states such as India, Pakistan, and Bangladesh that have strong military capabilities. Although these are not traditionally strong states such as the United States, they are strong enough to clamp down on militarized camps if they have the will to do so.

Then, in terms of the model, the relevant explanatory variable is the interaction term created by multiplying *separatism* with *complicity* to test whether separatism and state complicity is the combination that makes militarization more probable. The interaction term can tell us the effects of the four combinations of separatism and state complicity—separatism and complicity, separatism and no complicity, no separatism and complicity, no separatism and no complicity. Based on the arguments put forward earlier, it would seem that the separatism and complicity combination will explain militarization better than the other three combinations. Using the interaction terms is the appropriate way to analyze the contingency effect of separatism and state complicity.

Four models are presented in Table 4.2, with and without the two crucial variables (separatism, complicity) and the multiplicative interaction term. Model IV is the full model with the highest explanatory power judging by the log likelihood, the pseudo R^2, and the F-test.

For the logistic model with an interaction term, the coefficient and sign of the two variables of the interaction term indicate the effect of one variable (of the interaction term) when the other is 0, and vice versa. In this model, this means that when separatism = 0, state complicity has a statistically significant (at the 0.01 level) positive effect on the probability of militarization, and when complicity = 0, separatism has a statistically significant (at the 0.05 level) positive effect on the probability of militarization. Although the sign of the interaction term is negative, it does not mean that the separatism and complicity combination necessarily lowers the probability of militarization. Given that the logistic model is a nonlinear model, the effect needs to be further examined, which I do with the aid of predicted values and graphs, using the concept of covariate contribution (see Chapter 3). As it is a nonlinear model, the covariate contribution is not a constant but changes depending on the values. Therefore I examine the predicted probabilities of militarization stemming from state complicity and separatism at different levels of covariate contribution.

The range of covariate contribution in model IV is –16 to 1. The covariate contribution is –15.73 at the 20th percentile, –14.26 at the 50th percentile, and 0 at the 80th percentile. The predicted probability of militarization at these three levels is presented in Table 4.4.

The findings are counterintuitive but perhaps this is not surprising: given state complicity, the probability of militarization is higher when separatist elements are absent and lower when they are present, for most of the range of covariate contribution. This finding indicates that state complicity is one of

Table 4.2 Logistic regression for camp militarization

	Model I	Model II	Model III	Model IV
Constant	0.46(0.42)	0.028(0.436)	0.069(0.464)	−1.69*(0.699)
Separatism		2.11***(0.58)	2.22**(0.71)	13.60**(4.52)
State complicity	2.07**(0.70)		2.14*(0.85)	15.15**(5.38)
Separatism* complicity				−14.15**(4.45)
Aid	1.38e-07(8.01e-08)	1.81e-07(16e-07)	2.04e-07(1.73)	4.16e-07***(1.3e-07)
International organizations	0.26(0.52)	1.21*(0.51)	0.58(0.55)	0.472(0.76)
Alliance	−2.13***(0.41)	−2.08***(0.39)	−2.94***(0.46)	−7.86**(2.72)
Log likelihood	−63.67	−61.02	−56.75	−27.63
N	153	153	153	153
LR chi^2	63	68.3	76.83	135.08
P > chi^2	0.00	0.00	0.00	0.00
Pseudo R^2	0.33	0.35	0.40	0.75

*** p < 0.001, ** p < 0.01, * p < 0.05
Standard errors within parentheses
Dependent variable: Refugee camp militarization

Table 4.3 Predicted probabilities

Variable	Values	Predicted probability
Alliance	0	0.981
	1	0.922
	2	0.004
International organization	0	0.37
	1	0.48

the main factors in determining the militarization of refugee camps, which can occur even when there are no separatist tendencies.

At the 80th percentile of covariate contribution, however, the expected relationship emerges: the combination of separatism and complicity creates an 88 percent predicted probability of militarization—higher than 73 percent, the predicted probability when there is state complicity but no separatist incentives.

Thus for lower levels of covariate contribution, the predicted probability of militarization is higher when complicity = 1 and separatism = 0 (relative to complicity = 1 and separatism = 1), but for higher levels of covariate contribution (beyond the 80th percentile), the predicted probability of militarization is higher when complicity = 1 and separatism = 1 (relative to complicity = 1 and separatism = 0).

On the flipside, given separatism (separatism = 1), the predicted probability of militarization is higher when complicity = 1 relative to when complicity = 0, for the entire range of covariate contribution.

The expectations based on the arguments put forward earlier would predict the following ranked order of combinations of "separatism" and "state complicity" to explain militarization:

1 separatism = 1, complicity = 1
2 separatism = 0, complicity = 1; separatism = 1, complicity = 0
3 separatism = 0, complicity = 0

Figure 4.1 provides a graphical representation of predicted values for varying covariate contribution and reveals the following rank, from highest to lowest:

1 separatism = 0, complicity = 1
2 separatism = 1, complicity = 1
3 separatism = 1, complicity = 0
4 separatism = 0, complicity = 0

Taken together, it becomes clear that state complicity with militants is a consistent factor that explains the militarization of refugee camps.

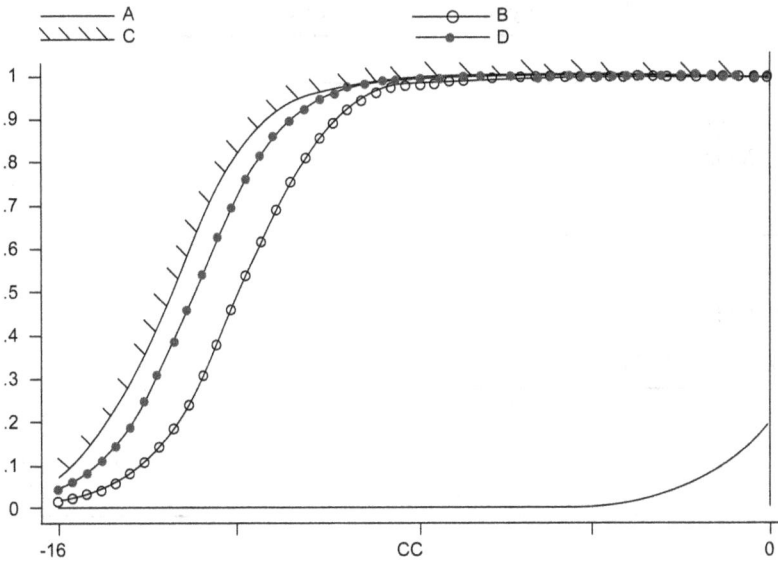

Figure 4.1 The predicted probability of militarization for varying covariate contribution based on the interaction between "separatism" and "state complicity"
Legend:
A: separatism = 0, complicity = 0
B: separatism = 1, complicity = 0
C: separatism = 0, complicity = 1
D: separatism = 1, complicity = 1

Related to state complicity is the relationship between the sending and receiving states, which is conceptualized by the variable "alliance" in the model. As might be expected, the predicted probability shows that when relations are bad and all else is equal (held constant at mean), the predicted probability of militarization is 0.92, whereas when relations are good, the probability is 0.004 (see Table 4.3). This provides evidence to support the notion of state manipulation of refugees for the purpose of bilateral/regional politics—when relations are poor (as is consistently the case in India and Pakistan), the receiving state has an interest in supporting and even instigating refugee militarization because refugee militants can undermine the domestic and political climate of the sending country. Conversely, a good relationship between the two countries will incentivize the state to prevent anti-sending country militarization in refugee camps.

The presence of international organizations, all things being equal (constant at mean), increased the probability of militarization from 0.37 to 0.49. This finding conforms to the notion of aid pilferage supporting militarization, whether aid is received directly from international organizations or through the taxation of refugees by militants. The presence of international

Table 4.4 Predicted probability of militarization for varying covariate contribution

When cc = −15.73 (20th percentile)

		Separatism	
		0	1
State Complicity	0	0.00	0.02
	1	0.09	0.06

When cc = 0

		Separatism	
		0	1
State complicity	0	0.5	0.73
	1	0.73	0.88

When cc = −14.26 (50th percentile)

		Separatism	
		0	1
State complicity	0	0.00	0.09
	1	0.31	0.20

organizations also signals to militants that there is money available directly, in the form of aid, and indirectly, in the form of the creation of a refugee economy that generates income and money flow in the camp areas.

Aid (in terms of millions of US dollars), however, has a very small but statistically significant (at all levels) effect on the probability of militarization. The coefficients and magnitudes for "presence of international organizations" and "aid," taken together, show that the dollar amount per se is not that important; rather, it is the "climate" and the possibility of a refugee economy that have a positive impact on the likelihood of the militarization of refugee camps. The analyses, thus, provide the basis to argue that the state is ultimately responsible for militarization within its borders.

Concluding remarks

In this chapter, I depart from the existing literature not in terms of the arguments per se, but in terms of the way in which they are framed: while much of the work presents rebels in camps in negative terms—calling for an end to humanitarian aid, for example—I frame rebels as representatives of refugees who have the desire and agency to bring about political change in their home country in order to make repatriation possible. I also provide empirical evidence, despite a very broad definition of state complicity, to provide support to an argument about state complicity that, thus far, has been theorized about but not tested empirically.

The fact that the militarization of refugee camps in India, Pakistan, and Bangladesh needs some form of state support is not surprising. After all, these states are strong enough to prevent militarization if they have the will to do so. So when the state ignores militarization, it supports militarization implicitly. What is counterintuitive is the notion that incentives for militarization need not come from the refugees themselves; the way in which the state ignores refugee activities as well as any form of direct instigation can bring about militarization as well, based on the data used here. The impact of the relationship between receiving and sending states further supports the notion of the strategic use of refugees to undermine or support the neighboring state whose repressive policies created refugees in the first place.

As noted previously, the analysis presented is limited, first because it is restricted to militarization in refugee camps only, based on a media-generated dataset, and second because the definition of state complicity is very broad, and it is in a very broad sense that state complicity impacts militarization. Can we tell a more general story about state manipulation of refugees in South Asia? Chapter 5 presents a more detailed analysis of the many forms of manipulation that have marred refugees' experiences in the region over the years.

Notes

1 Militarization is the proliferation of arms and weapons in refugee camps. Like protest, militarization requires leadership, which I refer to as a group or individual assuming the responsibility for recruitment, mobilization, and financing operations, as the *mujahideen* did during the Soviet occupation. Unlike protests, which aim to send a deliberate message to the authorities, militarization may be covert, with those outside the camps having limited or no knowledge of what goes on inside. As formulated in Chapter 3, a sense of deprivation underlies protests by refugees, which are aimed at drawing the attention of the authorities and the international community to their plight. In the event of militarization, motives are different. Refugees do not expect their grievances to be redressed or resolved. Instead, their goals and therefore the stakes are much higher—freedom, liberation, and independence, all of which signify strong cohesion and resolve among refugees/rebels.
2 Muslims who engage in jihad or holy war.
3 Kashmir provides the quintessential example of militarization to support a liberation struggle. However, I refrain from discussing the Kashmiri issue because they are not refugees; instead there are multiple claims to their nationality depending on which perspective one follows. The Kashmir issue remains a source of longstanding dispute between India and Pakistan and has acquired political strings that are unique to the crisis, although like many refugee situations it is a protracted crisis.
4 Interview conducted on October 20, 2008 in Bangkok, Thailand.
5 The Karen, Karenni, Mon, and Shan ethnic groups in Myanmar are also persecuted groups that flee to neighboring countries as refugees, but there is no denial of their citizenship or their claim to a state. The respective military units of these ethnic groups, the Karen National Liberation Army for example, have waged a low-scale war against the military junta over the years. They have not overpowered the military, but they have provided a constant challenge to the state framework that has ensured control over their territories.
6 Depending on the country of operation and the specific circumstances aid organizations face, such as the context of a given crisis, feasibility concerns, logistical issues, the role and reputation of local NGOs and IGOs, and the control of the receiving government, the receiving country may be in charge of aid money, or control might rest with local NGOs or UNHCR itself.

7 The state, however, may not be able to control militarization once it starts. Rebel operations and the proliferation of arms and weapons may become so efficient that the state loses control, in which case militarization can become a threat for the state. It may well be that states, by supporting militarization for strategic reasons, only succeed in generating an even more intractable problem for themselves. Hence, having already militarized for separatist reasons, rebel leaders can use their military capabilities against the state itself, if they consider such action useful.

8 As I argue elsewhere in this book, people from West Bengal (the state in India that hosted majority of the refugees fleeing East Pakistan/Bengal) openly supported militarization during Bangladesh's War of Independence because they felt that they were helping their Bangali brothers and sisters in their time of need. The government of India was thus forced to support the Bangali/Bangladeshi movement. Currently, people in the Indian state of Tamil Nadu are sympathetic to the cause of Tamils in Sri Lanka as well. Although there are studies to show that ethnicity does not impact civil wars (see Fearon 2004, for example), it may well contribute to militarization because of the loyalties that ethnic groups often share. Thus, shared ethnicity between groups within the host and refugee groups increases the likelihood of militarization.

5 Strategic manipulation of refugees

Is there something special about South Asia that makes it prone to protracted refugee crises? Why do these issues rarely get resolved? Why don't the countries involved discuss refugee issues and rehabilitation during South Asian Association for Regional Cooperation (SAARC) meetings or their many ministerial-level trips? Is it that countries are reluctant to discuss refugee issues for fear of straining bilateral relations? Do states have anything to gain from such crises? I argue that all three countries—India, Pakistan, and Bangladesh—have state-centric agendas that not only seek material gains but also attempt to reinforce nationalism and nationalistic ideals within their territories. They use discrimination as well as humanitarianism, as and when required, in order to sustain such sentiments. The ability to achieve perpetual domestic gains, materially and politically, through the strategic manipulation of refugees allows for unending refugee crises.

While Chapter 4 discussed the state manipulation of refugees in the context of militarization, this chapter provides a broader yet detailed analysis of the various ways in which refugees serve state interests, and whether these fall under "high politics" or "low politics." What the dataset used in Chapter 3 and Chapter 4 cannot convey is how the label "refugees" serves state interests as well. These chapters identified only those populations that are widely accepted as being refugee populations. However, as established in the Introduction, the word "refugee" takes on a very different meaning in the context of this region, whereby any migrant can be a refugee and any refugee can be an illegal immigrant. Also, militarization is often covert; although my research revealed some of the indirect ways in which militarization occurs, they are not included in the dataset used in the previous chapters owing to insufficient details and/or some of the claims being speculative. This chapter, thus, in addition to discussing how "mainstream refugees" may be manipulated, also identifies and analyzes the politics of identifying the same group of people alternatively as refugees, illegal immigrants, or citizens, depending on the interest of the state.

It is not the case that refugees are innocent pawns of state manipulation, however. Refugees allow themselves to be manipulated because, in exchange, they acquire some rights and/or material benefits to which they would not otherwise have access. Aid workers allege that large groups of Rohingya in Bangladesh are often driven by bus to polling centers by diverse political parties during elections in exchange for payment, as well as sometimes being recruited by terrorist organizations to carry out a number of illegal tasks (e.g., as gun runners or weapons-smugglers). At a time when the state cannot or does not protect them, refugees are forced to become pawns in the hands of local political actors and predators.

At times, state manipulation of refugees can actually serve the political interests of the refugees. India's "contain Sri Lanka" policy in the 1980s resulted in the arming of the LTTE, just as Pakistan's anti-Soviet policy in Afghanistan resulted in the arming of the *mujahideen*, both groups that owe their popularity to terrorism; in turn, such strategic support allowed the refugee groups to assert control in their countries of origin, Sri Lanka and Afghanistan, respectively. This chapter examines the various nuances associated with the state-refugee relationship in India, Pakistan, and Bangladesh.

India: the land of many ethnicities

While Indian politicians make all kinds of claims about Nehruvian democracy, the rights of minorities, and the role of humanitarianism in everyday politics, the ground realities are complex. Ethnolinguistic and religious fractionalization mean that people in different parts of India perceive refugees differently, depending on where the refugees come from. In turn, local perceptions of refugees may not correspond with the Central Government's position. Consequently, attitudes toward refugees cannot be categorized into "good" or "bad"; the push and pull factors create a range of intermediate levels that vary across groups and over time.

Tibetan refugees

The Tibetan crisis can be traced back to 1951, when Tibetan leaders were forced to sign a treaty dictated by the Chinese government. The treaty, known as the Seventeen-Point Agreement, guaranteed Tibetan autonomy and the practice of Buddhism while allowing the establishment of Chinese civil and military headquarters in the Tibetan capital, Lhasa. In response, an armed resistance began to take shape with the aim of preventing Chinese domination. The Dalai Lama's fears became a reality when Chairman Mao Tse-tung failed to honor the treaty's provision for autonomy, despite talks in 1954. By 1959 the armed struggle had spread across Lhasa, culminating in a revolt that was duly suppressed by the Chinese government.

Almost 80,000 Tibetans followed the Dalai Lama to India, where they set up a government-in-exile in Dharamsala, Himachal Pradesh, close to the Tibetan border. Camps were also established in the state of Karnataka and in Delhi. The Indian government set up education programs and healthcare services, provided the refugees with identity cards and travel documents, and also reserved some places for them in institutions of higher education. B. G. Verghese, a war correspondent at the time, wrote that

> these events greatly disturbed the Chinese and marked a turning point in Sino-Indian relations. Their suspicions about India's intentions were not quelled by Delhi's connivance in facilitating American-trained Tibetan refugee guerrillas to operate in Tibet and further permitting an American listening facility to be planted on the heights of Nanda Devi to monitor Chinese signals in Tibet.
>
> (*Times of India,* October 13, 2012)

Approximately 120,000 Tibetans live in India today, and their chances of repatriation are very low. Tibetans form the only refugee group in India to enjoy citizenship rights and residency rights in India (all other refugees are "illegal immigrants"). Those born in India gain citizenship as a birthright; others are eligible to receive residency and identity certificates issued by the Indian government and these serve as passports. The refugee camp in North Delhi is no longer called the Tibetan Refugee Camp; it is now known as the Tibetan Refugee Colony, flourishing with shops, restaurants, shrines—a smaller, Tibetan version of New York's Chinatown.

What explains the exceptional treatment that Tibetan refugees enjoy in India relative to other refugee groups? In order to explain India's welcoming stance toward Tibetans, two factors are important. First is the international reach of the Tibetan issue. When the Dalai Lama marched into India in 1959 with his entourage of 80,000, what could India do? Refusing them entry was not an option when the world was watching. It was an excellent opportunity for Nehru to show the world what he meant by humanitarianism in international cooperation. Hosting the Dalai Lama was a privilege; with that came international accolades and a credible position as a key figure in the NAM. India could thus capitalize on the Tibetan crisis to show that its foreign policy was actually based on liberal principles of cooperation. The question, then, is: did India not worry about upsetting the *Hindi-Chini bhai-bhai* ("the Indians and the Chinese are brothers") entente that it was simultaneously promoting?

The McMahon Line, which was drawn by the British in 1914 to demarcate the border between India and Tibet as part of the Simla Accord, has remained a bone of contention for decades. At the time Tibet was divided into Inner Tibet (under Chinese control) and Outer Tibet (which was to enjoy autonomy). The McMahon Line was considered to be the boundary between China and India, but China disputed it on the basis that Tibet had no authority to authorize the demarcation, as it was part of China in 1914 (K. Gupta 1980, 1982). The Chinese government posited that the Line of Actual Control, which coincides with the McMahon Line in the east but not in the west, is the true boundary where each state has "actual" presence.

These territorial concerns resurfaced during the mid-1930s, when India and China discovered that their maps differed. Gupta (1978, 1982) argues that the

McMahon Line was not based on a valid treaty. "Nehru was misinformed by the Historical Division, External Affairs ministry, New Delhi, when he was prompted to declare in Parliament (on August 13, 1959) that India's claim to the McMahon Line 'was firm by treaty, firm by usage.'" As such, "neither the Indians nor the Chinese have an uncontestable case on the border" (Gupta 1982: 1291). Guruswamy argues that

> on the surface it was all *Hindi-Chini bhai-bhai* and the practice of the Panchsheela philosophy, but underneath was the realization that the titles to large tracts of territory under the control of both parties were under dispute. The lid blew up when in March 1959 the Dalai Lama fled to India and was given political asylum.
>
> (2003: 4101)

Analyzing India's motives for hosting Tibetan refugees and the Dalai Lama in light of these simmering tensions disallows an interpretation of India's actions as purely humanitarian. In fact, one can see from this stance that India felt the need to counter the threat it perceived from China's growth by supporting a Chinese separatist group, as well as to assert its own power in the region. The cloak of humanitarianism provided the perfect pretext to undermine the Chinese government. At a time when India's military strength did not match China's, covert operations through the use of the Tibetan cause provided India with an indirect way of conducting warfare.

Allowing the Tibetans refuge gave India control over the disputed border areas because part of the territory falls under Tibet, which in 1959 established a government-in-exile in India. There is evidence to suggest that even during this period of *bhai-bhai* relations in the late 1950s, India increased its military presence in the border areas. One does not have to be a realist to recognize that such moves could and would be perceived as posturing at best and aggressive at worst, especially at a time when India was supportive of China's separatist group, the Tibetans. Objectively, therefore, there was a disconnection between what India claimed in terms of humanitarianism and Indo-Chinese friendship versus India's actions in terms of supporting Tibet and bolstering the military along the Sino-Indian border.

Accordingly, scholars such as Maxwell (1999) argue that the context of the 1962 war had already been set. "Unless Beijing surrendered to India's territorial claims to Aksai Chin and areas north of the McMahon Line, conflict was inevitable. China's military action in 1962 was reactive and pre-emptive, and that India suffered 'unprovoked aggression' is a self-serving myth" (ibid.: 905). Thus the granting of political asylum was not merely an act of generosity, but a strategic move to covertly gain and eventually assert power in the region.

Following the 1962 war, India "still talked about non-alignment, [but] in actual practice, it began to accept the bipolar reality of the world" (K. T. Hussain 1971: 2017). In effect, this meant that India became more consciously a power-seeking nation. Over time, as India and China made leaps in economic performance, trade between the two countries grew, as did competition. The world today expects these two nations to be the next superpowers. While they have worked together on international platforms to chalk out a space for the developing world—through BRICS[1], for example—India and China are rivals vying for regional dominance. India continues to accept new refugees from Tibet and, as mentioned previously, offers citizen-like provisions for Tibetan refugees. This, again, makes India appear magnanimous in light of Chinese brutality, but at the same time allows the country a pawn to manipulate when needed. Now that there is talk among the TYC about the futility of nonviolence and self-immolation, the rise of an armed struggle, covertly supported by Indian Intelligence, should not come as a surprise.

The Tamil Tigers

The Tamil refugee problem lies at the crux of decolonization. Ceylon (Sri Lanka) gained independence in 1948, but almost immediately, the prevalence of Sinhalese nationalism created a culture that treated the Tamil population as outsiders because these people had been brought in from India by the British in 1815 to work on the tea, coffee, and coconut plantations. Between 1956 and 1976 the Sinhalese government successfully suppressed periodic protests against anti-Tamil laws such as the proclamation of Sinhala as the only official language and the declaration of Buddhism as the state religion. Not surprisingly, perhaps, separatist sentiments grew among the Tamils, eventually giving rise to the LTTE in 1976. The following year, the separatist Tamil United Liberation Front (TULF) party won all seats in Tamil areas.

As a consequence, state repression no longer resulted in suppression: the creation of these organizations turned the movement into an armed struggle that over time began to use terrorist tactics. A series of "Eelam Wars" (wars of liberation) were fought in 1983, 1990, and 1995, amid an Indian intervention in 1983, failures in peace talks, the assassination of President Ranasinghe Premadasa in 1993, a suicide bombing at Colombo's International Airport in 2001, and thousands of Tamils fleeing to India to find refuge throughout the period.

An uneasy lull followed a ceasefire agreement in 2002, but violence flared up in 2006 and then again in 2008. After Velupillai Prabhakaran, the head of the LTTE, was killed during an "encounter" with the military, the organization accepted "defeat" and laid down its arms. Yet there are still 73,000 Tamil refugees in India, and several thousand elsewhere, who are afraid to go back to Sri Lanka for fear of persecution.

First, because of the continued repression of Tamils in Sri Lanka/Ceylon, stories of Tamils crossing over to India on makeshift rafts have been common since the early days of independence. The refugees traveled primarily to Tamil Nadu, where they were not only welcomed by local Tamils but received state patronage from the (state) government of Tamil Nadu. In fact, India's intelligence agency, the Research and Analysis Wing, along with the "Q Branch" of the Tamil Nadu police, supported, armed, and trained the LTTE to fight against the Sri Lankan military during the early 1980s (Gunaratna 1993).

That Tamil Nadu would support Tamil refugees comes as no surprise, given their shared ethnolinguistic heritage. The hosting of Tamil refugees provided three advantages for the Indian Central Government. First, India could portray itself as a welcoming and supportive host for refugees, an image congruent with the Nehruvian principles of humanitarianism at a time when the Congress was in power; second, the Central Government and Indian Intelligence could monitor the fervor of Tamil nationalism in the south that could give rise to irredentist sentiments in Tamil Nadu itself; and third, India could indirectly control politics in Colombo. Arming and training the LTTE meant that India could determine what happened in Sri Lanka. Seen through such a lens, India's hospitality was simply a facade; its support to Tamil refugees and the LTTE was driven by hegemonic interests and a desire to control the politics of "smaller states."

India intervened by sending the Indian Peace Keeping Force (IPKF), an apparently neutral force, to Sri Lanka in 1987 to disarm the warring parties and bring them to the negotiation table. The Tamils initially perceived this as a pro-Tamil move because of shared Tamil ethnicity. Soon, however, it became apparent that this was a military intervention by India on the part of the Sri Lankan state—the IPKF was embroiled in fighting the LTTE in northern Sri Lanka. Why would India fight a group that it had helped to arm and train? In the face of "rumors" that India was training and arming the militants, India had to prove its neutrality by fighting the LTTE. Although India sought to control Sri Lankan politics, it did not want to be seen as an enemy of the Sri Lankan state as this could potentially bring about an inter-state conflict. Also, there is the basic principal-agent problem: Indian Intelligence lost control over the LTTE. Unable to disarm the LTTE, the IPKF left in 1990 with no resolution for peace.

Back in Tamil Nadu, however, the locals remained loyal to their Tamil brothers and sisters, providing them with shelter and support, to which the Central Government did not object. However, Prime Minister Rajiv Gandhi's assassination by the LTTE in 1991 changed the fate of Tamil refugees. Some call this the beginning of India's "hands off" policy (Crossette 2002; Destradi 2012), but arguably, the outcome was devastating for refugees. In a country with no laws in place to protect refugees, discrimination became rampant. In order to stem militancy, refugee camps were relocated far apart. "Special camps" for militants were established that resembled harsh penitentiaries. Gandhi's assassination spurred a wave of nationalist sentiment that created an environment of hostility. Even if the Tamils in Tamil Nadu remained loyal, they did not want to act openly on such loyalties for fear of being labeled as traitors. It is not surprising that India opposed the UNHCR investigation of war crimes in Sri Lanka in 2007.

Thus, although the Tamils and the state government of Tamil Nadu feel a sense of kinship toward Tamil refugees from Sri Lanka owing to shared ethnicity, the Central Government's stance is more repressive because of its relationship with the Sinhalese government in Sri Lanka, on the one hand, and domestic politics, on the other. It is easy to see, then, how refugee protection gets bulldozed by politics, even when refugees have sympathetic allies in the receiving state.

Illegal Bangladeshis

The Hindu nationalist Bharatiya Janata Party (BJP) claims there are twenty million "illegal" Bangladeshis in India; according to the Indian Census of 2001 (Central Statistical Organisation 2005),[2] however, there were three million migrants from Bangladesh who resided in India. This number includes those in India legally and those who migrated during Partition and during the 1971 War of Independence (Shamshad 2008), which obfuscates the actual number of "illegal immigrants." At present, India claims that there are at least 200,000 Bangladeshi illegal immigrants in the northeast who have been forced into camps for their "protection" following a bloody confrontation in July 2012 between the Bodo tribe and the Bangali Muslims spurred by an act of criminality—an abduction and mugging. This event brought to the fore of national politics an age-old contention over illegal Bangladeshis, whom the BJP claims form a vote bank for the ruling Congress party. That explains, the BJP argues, the Congress's failure to complete the fencing of borders with barbed wires which began in 1989 (ibid.). One might also ask why the BJP did not complete the project during its tenure in power, from 1998 to 2004.

The first question to consider is: how valid are these claims of constant infiltration? Table 5.1 shows the decadal population growth rates in India, Assam, and the three districts in Assam that border Bangladesh.

The table shows that population growth during each decade before 1971 was much higher than the Indian average, accounting not just for a high birth rate but for immigration from what was then East Bengal/East Pakistan. Since 1971, however, the decadal growth rate in the bordering areas has been significantly lower than the national average. If we look at the three districts

Table 5.1 Percentage of decadal variation in population since 1951 in India and Assam

	1951–61	1961–71	1971–81	1971–91	1991–2001	2001–11	Muslim population
India	21.64	24.80	24.66	54.41	21.54	17.64	15.0%
Assam	34.98	34.95	–	53.26	18.92	16.93	30.8%
Dhubri*	43.74	43.26	–	45.65	22.97	24.40	74.29%
Dhemaji*	75.21	103.42	–	107.50	19.45	20.30	1.84%
Karbi Anglong*	79.21	68.28	–	74.72	22.72	18.69	2.22%

* Districts in Assam bordering Bangladesh.
Source: modified from Dutta 2012

in Assam that border Bangladesh, as shown in Table 5.1, two observations are particularly noteworthy. First, Dhubri has a high percentage of Muslims and a higher-than-national decadal population growth rate; second, the Muslim populations of the other two regions total less than 3 percent, yet these regions still have a high decadal population growth rate. The question that Dutta (2012) raises is: why would illegal immigrants go to only one of the three bordering states? Would "infiltration" not occur in all three districts? Politicians in India find it convenient to point to Dhubri when discussing illegal immigration, but ignore the evidence to the contrary.

What such definitions of illegal immigrants from Bangladesh ignore is the history of partition and migration in the region that predates independence, which has created pockets of ethnically similar people among other ethnicities. Today, Bangali Muslims make up 8.2 million of Assam's population of 26.6 million. The first wave of migration occurred when Assam was made a part of India's East Bengal province in 1905, with Dhaka as the capital. The second influx occurred throughout the 1940s, when the British relocated Bangali Muslims to farm the lands and increase food production (much like how Tamils were transported to Sri Lanka during colonial times), followed at the end of the decade by a third influx in 1947, during Partition. A fourth influx occurred during Bangladesh's War of Independence in 1971. Those who entered India after March 25, 1971, when Bangladesh declared independence, have been declared "illegal immigrants" by the Indian government in 1985 (Chatterji 2007; Van Schendel 2002; Tajuddin 1997).

However, there is little evidence to suggest that the 200,000 Bangladeshis who currently face deportation and possible statelessness entered India after 1971. The kind of opposition Bangali Muslims face today is not very different from how Sri Lanka treated its Tamil population. Interestingly, while India "understands" the plight of Tamils, it refuses to acknowledge the Bangali Muslim population in the northeast as its own.

What interest does India have in making the illegal Bangladeshis such a public matter? Does it not fear souring relations with Bangladesh when it portrays the Bangladeshi population in such negative language? It is precisely because this 200,000-strong population is not Bangladeshi that India is able to use such negative imagery without hampering bilateral relations. What supports this notion is Bangladesh's indifference to this issue at both national and local level even as it seems to be making national news on a regular basis in India, especially following the Bodo-Bangali conflict. No denouncements of anti-Bangladeshi atrocities appeared in any of the major newspapers in Bangladesh, though such denouncements are common when Bangladeshis, even illegal ones, are ill-treated, for example in countries in the Middle East.

However, what purpose does such negative imagery serve? For India, it is mostly about domestic politics and how the public perceives local conflicts. Why does the construction of the fence remain incomplete? Keeping the borders somewhat porous allows people to scream "infiltrators" every time a diversion is required, to focus attention on the ills coming into India. While some

Indian scholars find the construction of border fences offensive and even xenophobic (Pant 2007; Jones 2009), I spoke to a number of Bangladeshi researchers[3] who expressed frustration over such "politics." "Why doesn't India close the borders right now?" asked many. "Then they will see how many are actually from Bangladesh."

The open borders provide a pretext for suppressing minorities, Bangali Muslims in this case, and for creating an "other" that threatens local culture. Although local officials and authorities formally denounce communal violence, they actually promote it by assuming that the Bangalis are Bangladeshis by virtue of the fact that they are Muslims. The focus on the Hindu (Bodo)–Muslim (Bangali) divide disallows unity among different groups in Assam to engage in what many insurgent groups there seek—self-determination. Thus, the creation of the "other" not only serves as a "threat" on its own terms but also as a mechanism for divide-and-rule to prevent national disintegration.

The anti-Bangladeshi stance is not a specific issue, but part of a broader Indian agenda that seems to espouse nationalism based on "anti-someone" sentiments: in the north it's China, in the west, Pakistan, in the east, Bangladesh, and in the south, Sri Lanka. People from these countries are showcased as threats to Indianness, which can only be fought "unitedly."

At a time when Hindu nationalism is on the rise and the Congress, which is traditionally a centrist party, is arguably perceived by many as leaning to the right (Chenoy and Chenoy 2007), it is perhaps not surprising that anti-Muslim sentiments, whether anti-Pakistani or anti-Bangladeshi, find support among Indian politicians as well as the Indian masses. The need for a simplistic notion of nationalism—"unite against a common enemy"—along with the convenient denial of the history of migration serves the political agenda of politicians looking to gain political office in a multiethnic country where unity is difficult to come by.

That is not to say that illegal migration from Bangladesh is a myth. Porous borders make it difficult to study the exact number of illegal Bangladeshis in India, but there is anecdotal evidence to suggest that there are many. Some locals I spoke to in Delhi[4], for example, complain that many of the Bangla speakers are Bangladeshi but give the names of obscure villages in West Bengal as their places of origin, thereby masking their "true" nationality. Given that they speak one of the major Indian languages, Bangla; that there are many "Partition refugees" from what is now Bangladesh which can explain the variation in accents; and that they look "Indian," it is easy for illegal Bangladeshis to assimilate and "hide" among Indians. National identity cards are a new phenomenon, illegal immigration is "rampant," and there exist a large number of "Partition refugees" from the same region, making the process of identifying and verifying illegal Bangladeshis very difficult.

Anecdotal evidence from interviews[5] also shows (albeit inconclusively) that border guards are complicit in fostering this kind of migration. I heard the story of Aslam, who was deported from India, then detained at a detention center at the border. The border patrol gave him one meal, kept him locked up for five hours, and then told him to go back to where he came from (in India). There are also many news reports (*Daily Star* 2012b, 2012c) of border casualties where Bangladeshi herders and animal traders who cross over to India for petty business are captured, tortured, and killed. How representative are these stories? It is difficult to say. However, it is easier to understand how Bangladeshi illegal immigrants came to be perceived in mainstream Indian politics as a threat.

"Brave Bangalis": refugees during the War of Independence, 1971

The refugee influx into India in 1971 and the subsequent independence of Bangladesh can be traced back to a root cause—Partition. The partition of the Indian subcontinent in 1947 created two independent countries: India and Pakistan. Bengal was divided into two separate entities: West Bengal, belonging to India, and East Bengal, belonging to Pakistan. East Bengal was renamed East Pakistan in 1955. Most of the Muslim-majority areas of undivided India went to the newly created nation of Pakistan. This created a geographical anomaly, with Pakistan's two distinct and unconnected parts, termed West and East Pakistan, separated by India in the middle.

East Pakistan was more populous than West Pakistan, with seventy million people, but political power rested with the western elite in post-independence Pakistan, who refused to hear or address the grievances of the east. Such grievances were the basis upon which several political parties emerged in East Pakistan. A particularly dominant party was the Awami League (AL), led by Sheikh Mujibur Rahman, a highly charismatic Bangali leader, which drew millions of Bangalis to demand political rights. In 1970 Pakistan held general elections. The AL not only participated but won the majority of the seats, which would enable it to form the next government. The West Pakistan-based military government dismissed the results and, instead of handing over power to the elected representatives, embarked on military suppression and large-scale slaughter in East Pakistan to subvert the electoral results (Sisson and Rose 1990).

The final straw was the crackdown in East Pakistan on March 25, 1971, which left thousands of Bangalis dead, and led to the arrest of Sheikh Mujibur Rahman for treason. This provoked the Bangalis to declare independence and begin an armed struggle for liberation. Uncannily, only twenty-four years after East Pakistan's independence from Britain, another "partition" took place because the elite did not want to share political power.[6]

As the aggression of the Pakistani forces intensified, India had to open its borders to afford the (new) Bangladeshi refugees safe shelter. The state governments of West Bengal, Bihar, Assam, Meghalaya, and Tripura established refugee camps along the Indian border. The conflict resulted in a deluge of refugees into India and as the violence in East Pakistan escalated, an estimated ten million refugees fled to India (Sisson and Rose 1990). For a developing country like India, the resource pressures were immense.

The refugees were forced to go to India owing to Bangladesh's proximity to India. However, what started as a humanitarian effort soon developed political consequences, given the rivalry between India and Pakistan. There was already a conflict on India's western border over Kashmir. The Bangladesh "crisis" added another element; India had to calculate its moves.

Chapter 6 of this book deals with India's role in Bangladesh's war in more detail, but what is important to note is that, much like how Sri Lankan Tamils were initially treated in Tamil Nadu, Bangladeshi Bangalis in West Bengal enjoyed tremendous state support. Especially for those in West Bengal, welcoming co-ethnic Bangali refugees was a brotherly duty. In 2008 I conducted a survey[7] of fifty self-selected participants from refugee areas in West Bengal. All were sympathetic toward refugees and, although their impact was very visible, those I surveyed felt that supporting them was the right thing to do. Some were aware of training camps operating within the borders, but that too, they felt, was justified given the situation in Bangladesh. The state government of West Bengal, accordingly, was welcoming.

The Bangladeshi War of Independence was a source of pride among Bangalis in India, who despised the "weak, feeble, cowardly" stereotype imposed on them during the colonial period and even later to explain why the partition of Punjab was more bloody and violent than that of Bengal (James 2000). In a country where the Pathans and Sikhs were revered for being brave warriors and the Bangali *bhodrolok*[8] mocked for being overly "intellectual" and pedantic, Bangladesh's struggle showed that Bangalis, too, could fight for their rights and take up arms if necessary. This sentiment was expressed in songs broadcast on Akashvani Kolkata, Radio India's Kolkata station, to inspire refugees and guerrilla fighters. One song, for example, contains the lyrics: *Ma go, bhabna keno, amra tomar shanto priyo shanto chele, tobu aj shotru ele ostro haate dhorte pari, tomar bhoy nei ma amra, protibad korte pari* (Dear Mother, don't worry, we are your peace-loving sons, but if the enemy comes, we can take up arms; do not fear, we can resist). The war was an opportunity to prove, once and for all, that Bangalis are not cowards. To date, Bangalis, East or West, point to the war to say, "Yes, we can fight for change."

The war served Pakistan's purposes, too: Pakistan claimed that these developments were part of the Kashmir problem, arguably to justify what increasingly appeared to be genocide. The pertinent question here, though, is whether one can separate India's motive for supporting refugees from India's decision to send the Indian Army to assist Bangladesh.

It also is important to note that in this narrative, no matter what source one uses, the story that emerges is one of courage, righteousness, and support. It is difficult to reconcile this image with the current image that dominates the rhetoric of illegal immigrants as self-serving, rapacious, illegitimate, and unwanted. So what changed? Supporting Bangalis in Pakistan is very different from supporting Bangalis in Bangladesh. In the first case, India could use the refugee problem against Pakistan, domestically and internationally, to justify aggression in the face of Pakistan's oppression of civilians. In the latter, no such gains exist; supporting the migrants/refugees is burdensome without any strategic gains from doing so. Instead, the only way that India can gain from the illegal immigrant issue is through identifying them as outsiders, demonizing them and using them for the purpose of national unity.

Invisible Burmese

When one speaks of refugees in India, the Burmese are not the first to spring to mind. India's refugee stories are dominated by Tibetans and Tamils, followed by Bangladeshis. However, the population from Myanmar is 80,000 strong, according to the Chin Refugee Committee (CRC) in Delhi. Most are Chin, but since 1988 there have also been about 3,000 Rohingya who live predominantly in the northeast, in Mizoram and Manipur (although there has been a small influx into India since the 1970s).

The Chin population in Delhi numbers about 5,000, according to the CRC. They live in West Delhi—Vikaspuri, Uttamnagar, and Janakpuri—in makeshift conditions, mingled with the local population. Delhi is a desirable destination for this population because the only UNHCR office in India is located there; at a time when the Indian government provides no protection or support for the Chin or the Rohingya, UNHCR is their only beacon of hope. This has forced many Myanmarese refugees to trek across the country for days to reach Delhi in the hope of gaining refugee status.

Unlike the Tibetans in Delhi, who have a community of their own in a localized area, the Chin have nothing. What that means, in effect, is that this population has no support system. As the Chin do not speak English or Hindi, their existence is fraught with fear and uncertainty; they are exploited by locals sexually and/or economically, as often they are not properly paid for their labor. Chin refugees I spoke to in Uttamnagar, Delhi, in October 2012, complained of both. I spoke to women who fled Mizoram after being raped by local *gundas* or border guards. I met a woman who had in her lap a child born out of rape. In some cases these women face a situation far worse than the one they fled, but are unable to return for fear of ostracism.

UNHCR, according to the CRC, can provide identity cards to refugees following status determination, but the Indian government does not recognize them. That is, according to the government, with or without UNHCR documentation, refugees are foreigners who can apply for temporary visas or else remain as illegal immigrants.

Despite such conditions, the Chin are better off than the Rohingya, who are stateless. The Chin, at least, have been able to organize around the refugee committees and the Chin National Front. The Rohingya are fighting for a basic demand: citizenship. From their perspective, the Chin or any other refugee group in the region are far better off than they are, because they belong somewhere.

The Myanmarese in India are effectively invisible. Although 80,000 refugees is a large number in absolute terms, the state is uninterested in their plight. They serve no strategic purpose and their presence or absence makes little difference to the state. As Refugees International (2009) pointed out, the Chin work in the "informal sector" as maids, servants, cleaners, garments workers, and other jobs where identification is not required—a sector where there is still sufficient demand to keep the Chin employed without cutting jobs for locals. There is no state provision of services for this population and so they exist almost as free labor, working for a pittance.

Bangladesh: resource crunch

Bothersome Burmese: the Rohingya

The Rohingya crisis began in 1974 when the Burmese military government removed the Rohingya's citizenship, claiming that they were economic migrants who had traveled to Myanmar during British rule. This ethnic group is thus stateless, with the Burmese government not only refusing them citizenship but engaging in ethnic cleansing. Unlike in 1971 when India found its solution to the refugee crisis (more on this in Chapter 6) as a by-product of a military intervention Bangladesh has neither the military nor diplomatic power to force a solution on Myanmar (N. Murshid 2011).

According to UNHCR, the main problem that Bangladesh faces is that the districts of Teknaf and Ukhiya, which house many of the refugees, are among the poorest in Bangladesh. A panel report by Meghna Guhathakurta (2011), executive director of Research Initiatives Bangladesh, one of UNHCR's implementing partners, noted that "the average poverty rate in these two districts is 73% in Teknaf and 69% in Ukhiya. The literacy rate is 17% to 18% on average and the population growth rate is 3.1% with an average family size of 8" (ibid.: 2).

The report goes on to mention that the protracted nature of the refugee situation gives rise to the following problems:

1 New generations of refugees born inside Bangladesh have no access to education facilities, let alone citizenship rights.
2 The Bangladeshi state has become increasingly hostile, as is evident from the institutionalization of hate politics through Anti-Rohingya Committees and the closure of income-generating activities and educational provisions outside the camps.
3 The Rohingya have been criminalized.
4 There are no legal means for the Rohingya to generate income.

Thus, while taking refuge in Bangladesh saved their lives, the conditions the Rohingya have endured and continue to endure are dire. Bangladesh barely has the resources or the capability to provide even the basic necessities: the 330,000 Rohingya living in official and unofficial camps in Cox's Bazar, along Bangladesh's southeast border with Myanmar, live in cramped and unsanitary conditions in makeshift homes, with little access to clean drinking water and proper food. Moreover, they are subjected to maltreatment by local law enforcement authorities, as well as by locals who regard them as a threat and as competition for the limited resources and jobs in this already impoverished country. The perception that the Rohingya are there "forever," given their stateless status, only serves further to marginalize them. Guhathakurta described the situation thus:

> Since the refugee situation in this area is a protracted one, there is a general hostility from the host community. They are regarded as outsiders and hence with no rights, thieves, robbers and engaged in illegal activities like drug trafficking, and are often labeled as terrorists. Host communities at the local level have a love-hate kind of relationship with the refugees. They co-exist and hence they often cooperate, take pity, are sympathetic, exist in symbiotic relations e.g. giving them shelter in exchange for using their labor etc. But since refugees are in a desperate situation, they often get involved in illicit trade and other kind of exchanges, not unlike other poverty groups that live in the region. But they are singly targeted as being terrorists and traffickers.
>
> (October 15, 2012)[9]

Although the Rohingya refugees do not share ethnicity with the Bangalis, the Rohingya language is similar to a Bangla dialect known as Chittagongian, which is spoken in *Chatgaiyya* Division. Although native speakers of both languages can differentiate between the two, they have little trouble understanding each other. Having a similar lingua franca has allowed locals to be sympathetic and understanding and prevented them from identifying refugees merely as strangers from a foreign land. However, there are monetary incentives for locals as well.

The influx of international organizations, NGOs, and government offices involved in the protection of refugees has spurred an economy based around refugees. As encamped refugees are given rations and a small stipend, they too have become a market for locally available products. Local businesses, therefore, have benefited from the establishment of camps. When asked about their attitudes toward the Rohingya, some locals said that they were "a disruptive force that will destroy the land, the ecology, and spoil the local culture through pillaging of resources and promiscuity." However, beneath the overt dislike, the monetary incentives make locals tolerant of camp dwellers, who are officially not allowed to leave the camps but still manage to do so.

The state-level political debate highlighted by the media is not focused on camp dwellers, however. Whether the locals like it or not, the 30,000 registered refugees have managed to establish their rights in the area. It is the 300,000 unregistered refugees who are caught in the middle of all the controversy surrounding closed borders, discrimination, rape, and lawlessness. It is the unregistered refugees who really do not have any rights, and their numbers are on the rise as the Myanmar military continues to inflict violence on the Rohingya in Rakhine State. Guhathakurta added that the unregistered Rohingya

> do not have official assistance and hence have to literally scavenge for their livelihood. Often women who go to gather firewood in the forests are molested and raped. Only basic minimal services of health and sanitation are provided. During crises, as during the recent influx from Myanmar, they are completely at the mercy of security personnel.
>
> (October 15, 2012)

When fresh violence erupted in Rakhine State in June 2012, causing a fresh flow of people to seek refuge in Bangladesh, Bangladesh declared that it did not have the capacity to host more refugees and closed the border. This not only prevented people from coming into Bangladesh, but also prevented the Rohingya in Bangladesh from leaving. According to an aid worker in the camp area, the Rohingya have access to small arms and could have engaged in an insurgency in Myanmar. When the military began to attack the Rohingya in Rakhine anew, the Rohingya in Bangladesh made preparations to cross over to Myanmar to fight back. The closed borders and heightened security foiled such plans.

Does Bangladesh have any incentive to prevent an armed struggle in Myanmar? Recently, Bangladesh-Myanmar relations have been contentious over gas exploration in the Bay of Bengal: according to Bangladesh, Myanmar infringed upon Bangladesh's territorial waters around St. Martin's Island, but following an investigation, the maritime tribunal declared that the area lay within Myanmar's maritime boundary.

Did Bangladesh fear that it would be blamed for arming the Rohingya if they were to engage the Myanmar military, exacerbating the tensions between the two states? Or are the Bangladesh and Myanmar governments in tacit collusion to project state power by marginalizing the Rohingya? After all, the militaries of both countries claim that the Rohingya are terrorists—the Myanmarese military because it does not want to award citizenship to the Rohingya, the Bangladeshi military because more state funding for the military operating in the region will be made available if the refugees are found to be terrorists.

When Buddhist temples were burned down by "fundamentalists" in September 2012 (soon after the closure of the Bangladesh-Myanmar border) in Ramu, half an hour away from the refugee camps, a Bangladeshi MP asserted that the Rohingya were responsible for hate crimes against Buddhist minorities (*Daily Star* 2012a). The argument is that the Rohingya refugees could not cross over to Myanmar to protect the Rohingya from attacks by Buddhists in Rakhine; therefore, they attacked the Buddhists in their area as an act of revenge.[10] It is noteworthy that there is a significant "Rakhine" population in Cox's Bazar that has existed since before independence; unlike the Rohingya, they have assimilated into society in such a way that allows them to express their Burmese and Buddhist identities openly and confidently. (The

"Burmese" markets across the coastal region bear testimony to that.) No evidence has emerged as yet to prove or disprove the politician's claim, but locals I spoke to in Cox's Bazar (see Note 5) sang a similar tune: "One has to ask where all the ammunition came from. It is an open secret that the Rohingya have access to small arms," said one tea-stall owner.

The Rohingya are exploited for domestic electoral reasons as well. One finding that emerged during my fieldwork in 2008 was the manipulation of refugees to gain electoral leverage. The Jamaat-e-Islami party, especially, has often used religion to mobilize refugees, in addition to paying (bribing) them and/or promising them citizenship if elected. During the 2008 elections, the only districts where Jamaat-e-Islami succeeded were Chittagong and Cox's Bazar (Teknaf and Ukhyia fall under the latter). Although such claims are speculative, locals argue that part of the reason that Jamaat-e-Islami was successful in gaining two seats was through the mobilization of the Rohingya.

Owing to the fact that the Rohingya, especially those who are unregistered, are living in such desperate situations with very little hope for the future, they have been deemed the most vulnerable refugee group in the world by the US Committee for Refugees and Immigrants (USCRI). However, they are not only vulnerable; they are prone to manipulation by different groups and parties. Links to terrorist groups were forged because in the past the Rohingya were easily persuaded or bribed to carry and transport arms. "Because they have so little to lose and only something to gain, you can get unregistered Rohingya to do almost anything for money. They have been used as pawns for all kinds of illicit activities," said one aid worker who works with the Rohingya in the Cox's Bazar area.

The Bangladeshi state, for its part, continues its contradictory foreign policy. It engages in "quiet diplomacy" in its interaction with the Myanmar government, refusing to bring up the Rohingya issue in bilateral talks, but on the other hand, it continues to wage a low-intensity war against the Rohingya— including preventing Rohingya influxes, mistakenly hoping that this will force them to go back home and deter further influx.

Part of the reason for this kind of disengagement may be attributed to Myanmar's patrons, namely China and North Korea. With patrons such as these, Bangladesh treads a difficult path, unwilling to enter any kind of embroilment through a series of alliances. A confrontation with either China or North Korea is the last thing Bangladesh needs. "Myanmar pays little heed to the United States, the UN, and the European Union. Why would pressure from Bangladesh work?" asked a UNHCR employee in Kutapalang. The end result: continued repression of the Rohingya in Myanmar, creation of new refugees, and the protraction of the situation.

Interestingly, the Rohingya are skeptical of "democratic reforms" in Myanmar. Many think that a majoritarian system will only enable the Burman ethnic group to continue the suppression of minority ethnic groups. In fact, it has been claimed that Aung San Suu Kyi (along with others in the National League for Democracy—NLD) has brokered a deal with the military government: the NLD, they say, maintains an outward facade of openness while being part of a repressive pact. The fact that Suu Kyi has refused to talk about the Rohingya even when the topic is brought up serves to deepen their suspicion of her.

Bihari traitors

Also known as "stranded Pakistanis," the Biharis, like other Urdu-speaking non-Bangali Muslims from Northern India who settled in East Pakistan following Partition, supported Pakistan in its goal of suppressing Bangali nationalism in 1971. As they were Pakistani nationalists, they were opposed to Bangali nationalistic sentiments, which had gained popularity following the 1952 (Bangla) Language Movement that arose in reaction to discriminatory policies advocated by the Central Government in West Pakistan. They were, however, "stranded" in Bangladesh after Pakistani forces surrendered in 1971.

Following the division of Pakistan, approximately one million Biharis remained in Bangladesh. In mid-1972 the International Committee of the Red Cross estimated that 735,180 Biharis were stranded in sixty-six camps across Bangladesh; of these, about 60 percent wished to go to Pakistan. According to Bangladeshi government sources, this accounted for 539,669 persons (Ministry of Relief and Rehabilitation 1997).[11]

Pakistan, as a signatory to the Delhi Agreement of August 28, 1973, and the Tripartite Agreement between Bangladesh, India, and Pakistan of 1974, was under obligation to take back the Biharis (T.M. Murshid 2007). According to the Delhi Agreement:

1 The government of Pakistan "agrees initially, to receive a substantial number of (those who are stated to have opted for repatriation to Pakistan) non-Bangalis from Bangladesh."
2 "Thereafter meet to decide what additional number of persons who may wish to migrate to Pakistan may be permitted to do so" (Paragraph 3v).

The accompanying Memorandum of Understanding (MOU) further states that the government of Pakistan

agrees it will receive initially:

i   Persons who are domiciled in what was West Pakistan
ii Employees of the Central Government and their families; and
iii Members of divided families irrespective of their original domicile, and thereafter, 25,000 others who constitute hardship cases (MOU: Paragraph 1; Levie 1974).

According to paragraph 12 of the Tripartite Agreement that Bangladesh, India, and Pakistan signed in April 1974, the "Pakistan side reiterated that all those who fall under the first three categories would be received by Pakistan without any limit as to numbers" (quoted in T. M. Murshid 2007). Over the next two decades, Pakistan took back only 163,000 of the 539,699 Biharis who opted to go there, but that too was done in a way that favored the upper classes—those born in Pakistan to divided families and to military personnel and administrative officers, and who were not strictly Biharis (ibid.). However, small numbers have been leaving Bangladesh through indirect ways, without governmental or NGO support, as Table 5.2 implies.

During this period it was impossible for Bangladesh to arrive at a nego-tiated settlement with Pakistan except through diplomatic pressure. However, the Biharis' image as "traitors" was problematic. A new state that had emerged out of a secular Bangali nationalist movement had little to offer to a non-Bangali group that sided with the enemy. Even if the state did not take an aggressive stance, the local population viewed the Biharis with suspicion. Evidence that Biharis served as Pakistani spies and informants created an environment of hate; this was why UNHCR set up refugee camps for them in the first instance. The camps were meant to be havens in the midst of a hostile popu-lation. However, the government, fearing a backlash, was unwilling to allow extensive relief work to take place or the construction of permanent shelters.

To say the camps were havens would be a stretch of the imagination, espe-cially after UNHCR lost interest in the Biharis' plight. Initially, the interna-tional community feared annihilation, and therefore supported the creation of the camps. UNHCR realized that hostility did not necessarily mean that the Biharis had to fear for their lives or dread persecution, which meant that the Biharis did not count as refugees as per the 1951 Convention. Not surprisingly, international support waned.

When Pakistan was united, the Biharis in East Pakistan worked as small traders, clerks, civil service officials, doctors, and skilled railway and mill

Table 5.2 Numbers repatriated to Pakistan, 1974–98

Year	Number repatriated	Total to date	Left stranded
1974	108,754	108,754	470,000 (a)
1979		121,212	
1981	7,000	163,072 (b)	300,000 (c)
1993	325		237,440 (d)
1998	8,000	171,397	

Sources: T.M. Murshid 2007; Whitaker 1982: 16–17; Timm 1991: 10; Guest 1982: 25; International Committee for the Stranded Pakistanis (Biharis) in Bangladesh 1997: 4. The Committee estimated (a) to be 350,000 on the assumption that the total number opting for Pakistan was 470,000. See Ministry of Relief and Rehabilitation 1997: 3–4.
Notes:
(a) These people sought and failed to obtain repatriation by UN airlift.
(b) There has been a slow movement of population by other means, which accounts for this number; e.g., 41,860 were admitted to Pakistan via Nepal, Burma, and Sri Lanka.
(c) Concern, a relief agency working with the Biharis, estimated that by 1976 the number of camp inmates had fallen sharply to just over 300,000.
(d) There were 126,248 people living in camps, according to the Rabita Survey (1992, cited in Farzana 2008).

workers (T. M. Murshid 2007). The emergence of Bangladesh changed their fate almost overnight. In independent Bangladesh, Biharis took up work as cleaners, tailors, and barbers, although the camp areas became well-known for delicious Bihari kebabs as well.

The Biharis rarely protested or made any demands, except for repatriation to Pakistan. In 1979 50,000 Biharis attempted to walk to Pakistan but were turned back from the Indian border. They observed Pakistani national holidays and invited the Pakistan High Commissioner to attend their celebrations, but he never responded. They "went to see their Prime Minister" Benazir Bhutto when she visited Bangladesh in October 1989, but she refused to see them (T. M. Murshid 2007). Nawaz Sharif, during his tenure, promised repatriation, and there were hopes that his government and the Muttahida Quami Movement (MQM) would support the Biharis, given their support base among the Muhajirs (the Biharis would count as Muhajirs as well, once in Pakistan). However, even that remained a pipe dream.

In Bangladesh, the Bihari issue was never discussed in Parliament or at political rallies. For all practical purposes, successive governments turned a blind eye to the problem. Initially, a number of hate crimes were perpetuated against Biharis for being "traitors," but over the years even those stopped. Locals I spoke to in the camp areas in Dhaka in 2007 said that they felt no hate toward the Biharis, only pity. "Their lives are on hold and they face so many problems as it is. How can we be hateful toward them? They are the worst-off group in Dhaka City," said one *rickshaw wallah* who lived in a Mohammadpur slum. Consequently, there has been little dialogue on the Bihari issue at state or local level.

Bangladesh's post-independence negligence of the Biharis may have been a product of its aversion to conflict with neighbors. Addressing the Bihari issue would force Bangladesh to engage in (possibly heated) dialogue with both India and Pakistan, given that the Biharis originally came from Bihar (in India) but opted to go to Pakistan in 1947. As a new state that enjoyed support from India and was already in negotiations with India regarding the Bangali refugees there, Bangladesh may not have wanted to complicate matters by dragging in the Bihari issue. In addition, how could Bangladesh enter a dialogue with Pakistan—the state from which Bangladesh had just gained independence?

During my visit to Bangladesh in 2007, I met many Biharis who wanted to "go back" to Pakistan. They felt that Pakistan would eventually "do the right thing" and allow them to experience Pakistan as a state for the empowerment of religious Muslims. However, there was a generational divide: only the older among them harbored dreams of returning to the homeland one day.

The young generation felt very differently. Having been born in Bangladesh, it was the only reality they knew. Stories of Pakistan seemed like fairy tales to them. "We don't know anyone there; we don't even know the place. We have friends, family and jobs here. What will we do in Pakistan? Our future is here and we would like to tell the Bangladeshi government that at least those of us who were born here cannot be termed 'refugees.' I speak Bangla just as well as anyone else here," said twenty-five-year-old Mohammad Aslam.

In a somewhat surprising move, Bangladesh offered the Biharis citizenship during a political crisis, in 2007–2008. Following a military coup on January 11, 2007, a caretaker government was established under the direction of the military. Initially, given public support in Bangladesh for the caretaker system and its strong stance against corruption, civil society backed this. However, the mobile tribunal courts that were initiated for reasons of efficiency became a tool for intimidation. The Rapid Action Bureau (RAB) became a more aggressive paramilitary force, increasing the incidence of deaths from "crossfire" and "encounters." A delegation of Biharis sent a memorandum to the Election Commission, which was later communicated to the head of the caretaker government. It was in the midst of a host of anti-democratic actions that the government granted citizenship to the Bihari population.

How can the government's decision be explained? Previously, Bangladeshi citizenship had indeed been approved for Biharis on a case-by-case basis, but this was the first time that mass citizenship had been awarded to 300,000 Biharis.[12] The Bihari situation had stagnated for many years prior to 2007, with no hope of repatriation or Pakistani state support. Incorporating the Biharis into the population at a time when national identity cards were being implemented made sense logistically, as well as on humanitarian grounds. Many of the *razakars*[13] (traitors/war criminals) had grown old or died in the forty-six years since the war; neither the locals nor the state held the younger generations responsible for their ancestors' role during that period. Interestingly, the Bangladeshi state never tried to employ anti-Bihari sentiments for nationalistic reasons. In response to the Biharis' appeal for citizenship, the state, mindful that the general public would not be averse to such a decision, "did the right thing."

In placing this decision in the context of the brief military coup in January 2007, one could also point to Jamaat-e-Islami's infiltration of the military and the affiliation between Jamaat and the Biharis, based on orthodox religion and their shared opposition to the creation of Bangladesh in 1971.

Three interrelated questions arise. First, to what degree was the awarding of citizenship to the Biharis linked to the legal creation of a 300,000-strong voter base for the Jamaat-e-Islami in subsequent elections? Second, could not such a decision have been made democratically? Third, was the political parties' lack of opposition to the decision based on humanitarian grounds or fear for their own survival? Although such concerns are plausible, and there is evidence of an attempt to delegitimize political parties with the "minus-two" solution (that is, a transfer to democracy but with neither Sheikh Hasina or Khaleda Zia as heads of the two main political parties, the AL and Bangladesh Nationalist Party, respectively), there is little concrete evidence to make a strong statement—especially since the Jamaat-e-Islami did not fare well in the 2008 elections.

Nevertheless, the Biharis remain the only refugee group in South Asia to have gained unequivocal citizenship rights. As mentioned earlier, the Tibetans in India have rights too, relative to most others, but their citizenship rights are limited to those born in India between 1950 and 1987 (see *Namgyal Dolkar v. Ministry of External Affairs* (12179/2009 High Court of Delhi, India)). Interestingly, however, two very different circumstances led to the only two successful stories of integration. For India, China's economic growth and the competition for regional dominance played an important part in supporting the Tibetans. For Bangladesh, it was futility that led to integration: the realization that no other solution to the problem had presented itself, that it is better to have 300,000 productive citizens than 300,000 people who are deemed to be a burden to the state. What cannot be discounted, however, is the role of organized refugee groups such as the Stranded Pakistanis Youth Rehabilitation Movement and the Association of the Young Generation of the Urdu-Speaking Community, as well as the resettlement offices and refugee committees that advocated for the Biharis.

Today, interestingly, the Biharis still live in camps. The Bihari Camp in Mohammadpur, however, is more like a permanent settlement. Unlike the Rohingya camps, which are basically makeshift sheds with wicker walls and tin roofs, the Biharis' living quarters are made of concrete, with electricity and water supplies. There is an entire refugee economy in operation as well—from grocers, tailors, and beauty parlors to coaching centers and restaurants, all run by Biharis. Before, they used to pretend they were Bangali; now they can proudly claim to be Biharis. On October 21, 2012 the government approved the construction of a forty-five-storey apartment building for Biharis in Dhaka in order to help them to integrate within society and remove the stigma of a "camp address."

Pakistan: balancing public opinion and aid

Afghan refugees

Afghan refugees in Pakistan are the "odd ones out" in the South Asian context in many ways. While refugees in India and Bangladesh fled crises that originated from a single source within their home country (usually persecution by their own governments), refugees from Afghanistan in Pakistan fled foreign occupation and invasion in the 1980s and 2000s. Moreover, the foreign countries involved were superpowers, which meant there were almost no resource limitations constraining the war. Although the Afghans resisted, the ensuing scale of the violence led to the creation of a rapidly growing refugee burden along the Pakistan-Afghan border.

In the 1980s the Cold War and the bipolar international order "forced" the United States to become involved in Central Asia in order to maintain a "balance of power." Pakistan, a longtime US ally, gave US intelligence agencies access to its refugee camps. Afghan refugees became the US weapon of choice in the proxy war that was unfolding. Supported by Pakistani fundamentalists and financed and armed by the United States, the *mujahideen* were created in a sustainable fashion through the formation of *madrassas* that indoctrinated students into an orthodox, violent version of Islam. In no uncertain terms, the support given to the three million Afghan refugees was strategic. In the South Asian context, this was perhaps the most clear-cut case of refugees being manipulated to further US and Pakistani geopolitical objectives. Of course, the rhetoric used was of Afghan nationalism and the duty to support the oppressed, heedless of the fact that the war against communism had begun to create another threat: Islamic fundamentalism (Coll 2005). One wonders why US intelligence overlooked the potential threat of Islamism, especially after the Iranian Revolution brought orthodox Islam to the fore.

The sudden arrival of Afghan refugees did not please the locals. It "added to the volatile demographic situation in Karachi, whose citizens associated the 'drug and arms mafia' with these new refugees, most of whom were Pathans" (Haq 1995). At the same time, the refugee economy had a positive economic impact on Pakistan. More than 11,000 "bureaucratic jobs" were created and a plethora of businesses and NGOs sprang up to make use of the "monies cascading from the coffers of voluntary aid organizations and lucrative UNHCR contracts" (Dupree 1988).

It is, however, the bipolarity of the Cold War era that makes the manipulation of Afghan refugees during the Soviet occupation understandable in a way that it has not been since the 2001 US-led invasion and ongoing foreign occupation of Afghanistan. In the latter case, the narrative becomes much more complex and convoluted.

Following the US invasion, 2–2.5 million refugees fled to Pakistan despite sealed borders (Kronenfeld 2008; Human Rights Commission of Pakistan 2009) to become pawns once again in the game of international politics.[14] This time the refugees fled the Taliban government in Afghanistan in just the same way as they fled US bombings.

Once again, the first response to more Afghan refugees was not positive. Pakistan was unwilling to bear the brunt of yet another refugee influx at a time when its economy was floundering. As Duniya Aslam Khan, Associate Public Relations Officer with UNHCR in Islamabad, stated:

> The empathy level for refugees is going down as Pakistan's internal problems deepen. Locals accuse refugees of being involved in terrorist activities, also holding refugees responsible for the drug and weapons culture. Refugees are considered to be a huge burden on the economy as well. For the past few years, Pakistan has been juggling many internal issues which include financial problems, security issues, internal displacement caused by natural disasters—the 2005 earthquake, the floods in 2007 in Balochistan, the 2008 earthquake in Balochistan, the 2009 crisis in Swat with internally displaced populations, floods in 2010, 2011, 2012—and the

ongoing law enforcement operation against the insurgents in the northwest of the country.

(October 9, 2012[15])

Not surprisingly, Pakistan's position has often seemed contradictory. On the one hand, President Pervez Musharraf pledged to support the US "war on terror"; on the other, Pakistan's largely Muslim population and the Pakistani Taliban, despite their negative attitude toward refugees, both perceived (and still perceive) the US presence as illegitimate. Scholars speculate that Pakistan's autocratic military regime facilitated US support in exchange for the lifting of sanctions and millions of dollars in aid; a democratically elected government may not have been able to support the "war on terror" in a similar fashion (Stone 2004). Pakistan's dualism became clear later when the fugitive al-Qaeda leader Osama bin Laden was found and killed in Abbottabad, Pakistan, near a military base.

On the face of it, Pakistan was a US ally fighting the Taliban and a good host to refugees. Duniya Aslam Khan described the situation to me:

> Refugees don't live in camps anymore. They are now called "refugee villages" because through years of expansion, these camps have grown enormously in size and the tents have been replaced by traditional mud houses. We have some eighty refugee villages in Pakistan, where there are schools providing free elementary education, free basic healthcare facilities, and water supply schemes. Refugees don't have to pay for the land or houses; the government of Pakistan provided land for the establishment of the refugee villages. Conditions, of course, are not ideal but satisfactory.
>
> (Islamabad, October 9, 2012)

The refugees provided the context for the inflow of aid money; Pakistan's support enabled the camps and refugee villages to become bases for militants from which to sustain the war effort in Afghanistan. Pakistan's position of political support, albeit covertly, for the Afghan cause had partly to do with the influence of the Pakistani Taliban and partly to do with the ability to exercise control over Afghan politics. Afghanistan, as the gateway to Central Asia, offers ample material benefits, not least of which is access to oil and gas pipelines from Turkmenistan to the Arabian Sea (Matinuddin 2000).

The US drone regime heralded a new ideological element, as many Pakistanis began to perceive the drone incursions as attacks on Pakistani sovereignty. Well-known politicians such as Imran Khan of Pakistan Tehreek-e-Insaf (PTI) called for unity to fight imperialism in light of the unmanned drone attacks. Now that Pakistan has reinstated democracy, it has become difficult for the Pakistani state to support what is increasingly regarded as an illegitimate, if not illegal, presence in Pakistan and Afghanistan. Such aerial strikes, not unlike the US bombing of Cambodia in the later days of the Vietnam War, serve to recruit insurgents among the refugee population and the Pakistani population.

While Pakistan's support for Afghan refugees in the 1980s was largely influenced by Cold War politics, the scenario in the post-9/11 era is more complex. Local Pakistanis tend to regard Afghan refugees negatively owing to the competition which they provide, but many Afghans and Pakistanis share cultural and tribal bonds. There are material interests to be realized from the refugee economy and through gaining control over Afghanistan's national politics, but at the same time, camaraderie, compassion, and shared victimization have helped the the Pakistani state to overlook the fact that the camps serve as bases for armed struggle among the refugee population.

While India and Bangladesh have to be cognizant of regional politics and power plays, they do not need to be mindful of superpower politics in the way that Pakistan has had to. As the United States is, arguably, the world's only superpower (despite an emerging multipolar system), it is difficult for Pakistan to assert itself and its interests without taking into account its alliance with that country. The refugees in Pakistan, consequently, bear the brunt of the multilevel theatrics involved in Pakistan's international relations.

Partition refugees

Partition was intended to create a safe homeland on the basis of religion; instead it killed 1.5 million people and displaced another fourteen to seventeen million. The irony doesn't end there. Sixty-five years after Partition, many individuals and their families are still labeled "refugees" in their new homelands, and many continue to live in refugee colonies. Manto's words ring true even today: "India was free. Pakistan was free from the moment of its birth. But man was a slave in both countries, of prejudice, of religious fanaticism, of bestiality, of cruelty (1987: 6)."

The India-Pakistan border remained open until 1951 to allow for resettlement. Six million non-Muslims moved from Pakistan to India and eight million Muslims moved from India to Pakistan.

> Hindus and Sikhs "had" to leave for "their" nation India, and Muslims were driven out to their "own" Pakistan. A perverse logic that guided this forced migration was that room had to be made for the incoming refugees from the other side.
>
> (Kaur 2006: 2222)

So, more refugees were created in the name of hosting refugees. Although in the collective imagination of South Asians, the story of Partition is one where people were united in grief and misfortune, trudging hundreds of miles on foot, that is a misrepresentation. "Upper class and upper caste migrants— who flew down to safety [or whose] household belongings and bank accounts were transferred through official means" were not subject to the hardships that the majority suffered (Kaur 2006). This class distinction is important because it set the precedent for how migrants are treated in their new homes decades later. Rich, upper-class, educated migrants from Karachi formed the social and economic backbone of Delhi; no one would call them refugees. It is the poor, the underclass, the subalterns who face such discrimination, even today.

When Partition refugees are discussed in the literature or in popular media, several groups of underclass peoples are identified, the most prominent of which are the Muhajirs in Sindh, Pakistan, and the Bangalis in West Bengal, India (Talbot 2011; Haq 1995; Mukhopadhyay 2007; Sengupta 2007; Puri 2007; Marsden 2005; M. Rahman and Schendel 2003). Thus, a closer study of the division of the Punjab and Bengal is warranted.

In the Punjab, nearly twelve million Sikhs, Muslims, and Hindus were displaced and one million lost their lives (Zolberg et al. 1989). In Bengal, the Kolkata riots spurred the first waves of migration in 1946, prior to Partition (Chatterji 2007; P. K. Chakrabarty 1999).

> The western and eastern borders experienced different dynamics of Partition. Till 1951, the flows on the western border were almost three times the size of the flows on the eastern border. The west in general received about 10.7 million people while the east received about 3.2 million. Moreover, while there was greater movement out of India than into it along the western border (Pakistani Punjab received about twice the number of migrants as compared to Indian Punjab), it was the opposite along the eastern border—West Bengal received about twice the number of migrants as compared to Bangladesh.
>
> (Bharadwaj et al. 2008: 43)

Figure 5.1 shows in very concrete terms that (1) the migration to West Pakistan from India was twice the size of the migration from West Pakistan to India; and (2) the migration to West Bengal (India) from East Bengal (Bangladesh) was twice the size of the migration to East Bengal from India. In effect, migration flows resulted in a rise in net population in West Punjab and West Bengal, but caused a decrease in population in East Punjab and East Bengal. It is no surprise, then, that the populations most susceptible to discrimination in the new territories were the Muhajirs—migrants from East Punjab to West Punjab, and the Bangals—migrants from East Bengal to West Bengal. The refugees were most visible in West Punjab and West Bengal owing to their sheer numbers. The rich and the educated were able to settle in their new homelands easily enough thanks to the material and social capital that helped them to assimilate; at best they exemplified the ease of migration, and at worst they were hardly noticed in their new communities. The poor, by contrast, found it difficult to assimilate. They began to cluster together in their new cities, Kolkata and Karachi, and occupy what would eventually be labeled "refugee areas"—economically depressed areas with high levels of poverty, unemployment, and homelessness.

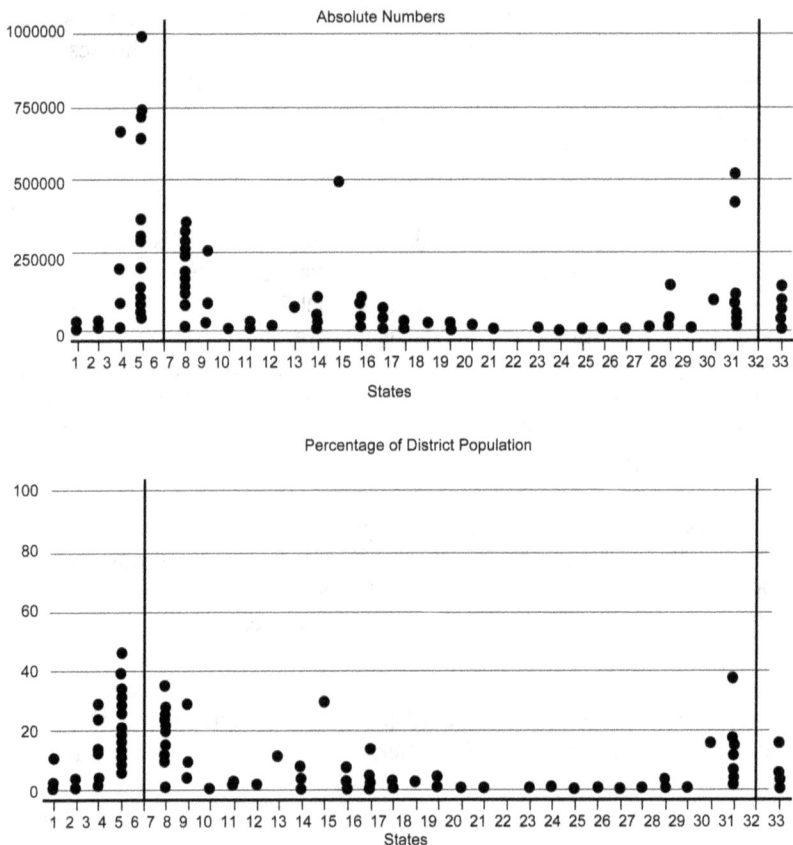

Figure 5.1 Inflows in terms of absolute numbers and percentage of district population
Source: Bharadwaj et al. 2008.

In the case of the Bangals, a new dialect also called Bangal emerged which was an amalgamation of different dialects of Bangla—Chittagongian, Sylheti, Mymensinghi, and so on—spoken in different districts of the East from where refugees came. Such distinctions from the rest of the people in the new territory would set them apart for years to come.

Although identified as refugees even today, the Muhajirs, who by 1951 constituted 55 percent of Karachi's population (Haq 1995) were able to organize politically and form the Muhajir Quami Movement (MQM, later renamed the Muttahida Quami Movement), first in 1978 as a student organization and in 1984 as a fully fledged political party. In subsequent years there were shifts within the MQM and factions emerged, but they were able to project political power through participating in elections and in a coalition government with the Pakistan Muslim League in 1990. As of 2012 the MQM held twenty-five seats in the National Assembly. Having this ability to mobilize politically is in direct contrast to the Bangalis, whose cohesion did not have a political platform but found expression in local football, where the Bangali team, East Bengal loved to play Mohun Bagan, the "local" (Ghoti) team. Bangal pride in West Bengal also rested partly on claims to intellectual superiority reinforced by Amartya Sen's Nobel Memorial Prize in Economic Sciences, for example.

The question is: who benefited from such groupings and cliques? Initially, refugees themselves gained from these labels, which served to provide a shared identity at a time when they had none, unlike everyone else in their new homeland. Such labels helped to bring together populations from different parts of East Punjab or East Bengal to forge a common front. The terms Muhajir and Bangal, which refer to refugee status, served two contradictory roles, however. These groups could place themselves in a historical context as part of a long narrative that brought them to their new homes. That Partition refugees still enjoy relating stories of Partition and of pre-Partition grandeur attests to this notion. On the other hand, the refugee label identified them as outsiders who did not have a shared past with the locals. For all practical purposes, their lives had just begun.

This contradiction has allowed the refugees' respective states to use them as scapegoats. The Muhajirs, for example, have been identified as encroachers, an image that serve to "unite" the rest of Pakistan on the basis of anti-Muhajir sentiments. The existence of MQM facilitated group discrimination after allegations that the MQM had terrorist links in the 1980s (Haq 1995; Alavi 1989; A. Hussain 1987). The Bangals, for their part, often bore the brunt of Kolkata's demise, both economically and in terms of cultural prominence. According to popular perceptions, it was not thirty years of communism that dulled West Bengal's economic potential, or Hindi cultural hegemony that led to Bangla's decline in popularity; it was the overwhelming number of refugees that drove West Bengal into stagnation (Chatterji 2007; N. Chatterjee 2002; Bandyopadhyay 1999; P. K. Chakrabarty 1999).

Yet such labels remain, because the groups themselves want them to remain; while they were once used as a tool for discrimination, they have now become a source of pride as well. Bangals speak Bangal with pride, even when they know how to speak *shudhho Bangla* ("proper" Bangla); they have created an identity and language that are wholly their own—which they share with no one in West Bengal/India or Bangladesh. Muhajirs claim with pride to have invested "emotionally" and "materially" in the idea of Pakistan and in "nation-building," having sacrificed much in the process of migration (Toor 2011: 57). Thus, as odd as it may sound, Partition refugees are still refugees!

Conclusion

Although I used a state-based approach to discuss refugees (in terms of identifying refugees in each state and analyzing state responses to them), some of the cases literally spill across borders, which renders the state-based approach somewhat useless. Take the Bangali Muslim refugees, for example. The "immigrants" in northeast India (Assam primarily) and in the Rakhine (Arakan) state of Myanmar are termed "Bangali Muslims," as if that alone implies they are from Bangladesh (illegally) and as if the existence of Bangali Muslims is ahistorical—denying the colonial legacy that took them to the frontier region of South Asia in the east. Part of the reason may be the desire to construct, in each case, a nationalist narrative that begins with decolonization and independence. Paradoxically, by denying the colonial past out of nationalist sentiments, both India and Myanmar continue to create "others" from among their populations; the slogans of "unity in diversity," which Indian nationalists like Nehru propagated and Myanmar's democratic reformers advertise today, seem to be pure rhetoric.

This brings us to colonization itself, which was responsible for much of the initial population displacement in South Asia (and elsewhere, for that matter).[16] When we examine cases of "statelessness" in particular—such as with the Bihari, the Rohingya, Bangali Muslims in northeast India, and Tamils in Sri Lanka—we realize that such issues have risen from colonial or even precolonial setups. That newly independent countries have not been able to include them in their respective national narratives speaks to the hypocrisy of nationalism, which continues the colonial practice of divide-and-rule. It was not only British colonialism that Indian nationalists opposed at the "moment of departure," however; nationalist scholars such as Bankim Chandra envisioned independent India as a nation of Hindus, proclaiming that the Muslims were invaders (P. Chatterjee 1986). Therefore, perhaps, it is not so surprising that Muslims in India have to, or at least feel the need to, justify and defend their existence and overtly proclaim their loyalty to the state. A discussion of Muslims in India is beyond the scope of this book, but what this highlights is the persistence of nationalist narratives constructed during the period of decolonization. Such narratives, by excluding certain groups or populations, have facilitated the almost perpetual denial of rights to these populations and enabled the state to use these groups as strategic pawns to create unity in a nationalist framework, attain regional dominance, or simply gain leverage in its interactions with its neighbors, as the cases identified in this chapter show.

Notes

1 BRICS is an informal grouping of large emerging economies, comprising Brazil, Russia, India, the People's Republic of China, and South Africa (together accounting for some 20% of global gross domestic product).
2 Published in 2005, it is the latest census available.
3 I spoke to researchers at several think tanks based in Dhaka on August 13, 2012, soon after the violent clash between Bodos and Bangali Muslims in Assam.
4 Discussion held with academics at the School of International Studies at Jawaharlal Nehru University on January 29, 2013.
5 Interviews conducted during the week of October 22, 2012 in Cox's Bazaar, Bangladesh.
6 There are more similarities between this event and the creation of Pakistan (or Partition). Each was preceded by a growing middle class, restriction of opportunities, increased competition, and struggles over territory and economic disparity

which created grounds for nationalism based on ethnicity/religion. The language of political mobilization, however, was in terms of recreating an ideal: the establishment of the *Khulafa-i-Rashidun* ("period of the rightly guided caliphs") in Pakistan, and of *Shonar Bangla* ("Golden Bengal") in Bangladesh. In both cases, there was deep suspicion of the "other." The last straw, in both cases, may well have been the experience of violence, such as the Partition riots of the 1940s and the army action in East Pakistan that began on March 26, 1971 (T. M. Murshid 2007).

7 I conducted an online survey via social networking sites during the period June to September, 2008.

8 Literally translated, *bhodrolok* means "polite man," but it used to denote the emerging middle and upper-middle classes in colonial Bengal who focused not only on material riches but on education to enrich the mind.

9 Interview conducted in Dhaka, Bangaldesh, on October 15, 2012

10 The same kind of argument was used to attack Hindus in Bangladesh and Pakistan after Hindus demolished the Babri Mosque in Ayodhya, India.

11 Whitaker (1982) puts the number at 534,792.

12 There were some nuances. The Biharis were divided into three categories. Category 1 consisted of those who were born in Bangladesh; Category 2 consisted of those born prior to 1971; and Category 3 consisted of those who self-identified as Pakistanis and did not want Bangladeshi citizenship. Citizenship was granted to the first two categories in phases. Citizenship remained optional for those in Category 3.

13 In 1971 the *razakar* formed the Pakistan Army's paramilitary force in East Pakistan along with al-Badr and al-Shams. Today, it is used in a broad sense to mean traitors and collaborators during the 1971 war.

14 Actual numbers, however, are disputed because the official statistics provide a stock value as opposed to a flow value. Hence we only have the cumulative population size at a given time. Looking at annual changes can be helpful, but concerns over the discrepancy between registered and unregistered refugees and a high birth rate among refugees seem to sustain the mystery over actual numbers (Kronenfeld 2008; Koser 2011).

15 In e-mail communication with the author.

16 The British promised a free Tibet, a free Karen state, and a free Chin state. They took Tamils from India to Sri Lanka and Bangalis from Bengal to Assam to work in plantations and fields. Partition, which was negotiated and not democratically decided, resulted in arbitrary borders drawn with no thought given to indigenous populations or ethnic groups.

6   India's military intervention in East Pakistan, 1971

On July 25, 2011, Sheikh Hasina, the prime minister of Bangladesh, post-humously awarded Indira Gandhi, the former prime minister of India, the Bangladesh *Swadhinata Sammanona* (Freedom Honor) for her "outstanding contributions to Bangladesh's Liberation War" (Habib 2011). At this juncture of the book, India's "outstanding contribution" may appear to be that it acted in a "humanitarian" manner to help Bangali refugees and to prevent geno-cide. While India's role cannot be denied, it must be noted that in the winter of 1971, at a time when the Cold War was affecting relations among states and military intervention was largely a tool for great powers, many regarded India's decision to intervene militarily in East Pakistan as an aggressive move.

Many questions arise as to India's intentions. Was India's involvement on December 3, 1971 an act of aggression or retaliation against Pakistan for an incursion on the western front? Or did India really intervene on humanitar-ian grounds to stop "a second Holocaust," as Indira Gandhi's many speeches suggest? Were concerns over hosting refugees an issue, as India's various representatives to the United Nations and ministers pointed out time and again during the nine-month war? Were there security issues arising out of the fact that India was hosting militarized training camps for the freedom fighters?

The literature suggests that bordering host countries may intervene mili-tarily in refugee-producing neighboring countries in an attempt to stem and reverse refugee flows (Dowty and Loescher 1996; Posen 1996; Teitelbaum 1984). Vietnam, for example, intervened militarily in Cambodia in 1978 after it had supported refugees fleeing the Pol Pot regime since 1975. The Vietna-mese had other reasons as well, such as putting on a show of power to Thai-land and ending the genocide in Cambodia (Dowty and Loescher 1996).[1] However, the refugees and the need to repatriate them cannot be overlooked.

More recently in 2008, Ethiopia sent troops into Somalia, "fearing" attacks from Islamic forces there. The fact that Ethiopia hosts 258,000 Somali refugees is a pertinent factor. As the intervention failed and Ethiopia was forced to withdraw its forces, it could not reap the benefits it had anticipated. Indeed, the situation worsened as the conflict produced more refugees. Hypothetically, a successful intervention could end the conflict in Somalia, and this might enable refugees to return home.

The Indian case has been mentioned in the literature in the context of hosting refugees by Salehyan (2008), Dowty and Loescher (1996), and Teitelbaum (1984), all of whom present Indian intervention in Pakistan's "civil war" as not just a response to refugee flows, but more importantly, as India seizing the opportunity to divide Pakistan. Although this intervention took place over forty years ago, there appears to be little understanding of its causes or, more specifically, its timing. This chapter therefore focuses on the Indian case to provide an in-depth analysis of the motives for intervention.

This chapter, thus, explores the various arguments—shared ethnicity, irredentist tendencies, lack of strategic importance, regional hegemony—to understand the motives behind India's apparent aggressive behavior, as it was perceived by the international community at the time. Through an analysis of the speeches of key actors and the reactions of ordinary men and women, I argue that the lack of international interest and strategic importance, combined with the heavy burden of hosting ten million refugees, explain the timing of and impetus for military intervention, an action whose repercussions are seen even today.

Methodology

I analyzed the motives behind India's support for and intervention during Bangladesh's War of Independence in 1971. My findings were obtained from three sources: surveys and interviews; newspaper archives; and speeches by key actors, including different ministers, the Indian prime minister, and India's representatives at the United Nations.

During a three-month period in 2008 I conducted two separate surveys on Bangladeshis and Indians who were alive during the 1971 war. All participants in the surveys were above fifty-five years of age and were living in India during the war. In terms of relevant sample size, I interviewed forty Bangladeshis who were living in India during the 1971 war as refugees and fifty Indians who were locals in India during the same period. (For brevity, I refer to the survey of Bangladeshis in India in 1971 as the Bangladesh Survey and that of Indians as the India Survey.)

The Bangladesh Survey was conducted in Dhaka, Bangladesh. Residents of alternate houses on two major roads in a central *thana* were interviewed. This area was chosen after studying the latest census report owing to the diversity of its population in terms of income levels, migrant populations, and gender.

The India Survey was conducted online using various social networking tools to make the survey available to Indian communities across the globe. This method was employed because a pilot study in West Bengal indicated that 2 percent of the pilot sample were living near camp areas and were thus unable to add anything substantive to the study. As there were no geographic barriers to the online survey, more "effective" respondents were able to participate. Of course, the sample is self-selected.

It is difficult to access newspapers and speeches dating from 1971 in Bangladesh, primarily because the main archive, located in the Dhaka Public Library, was burned down during riots in 1990. However, I was able to access two compilations of local and international newspapers that provided coverage of the war. The first is *Bangladesh Genocide and World Press*, compiled and edited by Fazlul Quader Quaderi, which he self-published in Dhaka, Bangladesh, in 1972. The second is a personal compilation of newspaper clippings dating from 1971 (from East and West Pakistan as well as international media reports) maintained by Sheikh Ahmed Jalal, now held at the Liberation War Museum in Dhaka, Bangladesh. The speeches were archived at the National Archives in New Delhi in 1972 before being released by the Indian Ministry of External Affairs and published as *Bangladesh Documents* (Singh 1999).

Some explanations for India's intervention

Camp militarization

During the War of Independence, the Bangalis of East Pakistan were fighting for self-determination. Hence, the kind of rebellion in which the refugees in India were engaged had little to do with India's treatment of refugees or the living conditions in camps, although these were very poor. Given that a government-in-exile was formed in Agartala, India, which was also the base of operations, it was, perhaps, almost inevitable that the nearby areas would become militarized.

All forty respondents to the Bangladesh Survey were frank about the existence of armed bases in India. In fact, ten of them had been "soldiers" in the East Pakistan regiment of the Pakistan Army—the Mukti Bahini who crossed the border several times and thereby did not have a permanent place to stay. Others had been volunteers who worked in the camp hospitals as aides. All respondents above the age of sixteen in 1971 had participated in the war effort in one way or another, whether working with Radio India's Swadhin Bangla Betar Kendra (Independent Bangla Radio Station) to spread news about the war or as journalists, broadcasters, teachers at camps, and so on. The war was not fought solely by the former Pakistani military—literally everyone participated, according to the respondents. All were aware of the existence of training camps in India alongside the government-in-exile. Rebels, therefore, did not have to operate out of refugee camps per se. They used secluded jungles near the borders as training areas.

The respondents to the India Survey who lived in areas close to refugee camps knew of the training camps as well. While most (forty out of fifty respondents) felt that the camp and adjacent areas were dangerous, they did not deem the bases to be a security threat. On the contrary, many of the respondents felt that the bases were necessary to continue the war efforts in East Pakistan.

Although the refugee camps themselves were not militarized, they served as fertile recruitment grounds. The *Far Eastern Economic Review* ran a story on militarization that observed: "Eyewitnesses report the Mukti Fauj [Liberation Force] is increasingly better organized and claim that more and younger men are joining it. An intensive recruitment drive is on in the camps to enlist all men and boys from the age of 14 up" (August 28, 1971: 80).

The question that becomes relevant is whether militarization played any role in India's decision to intervene. Militarization is a negative externality. If better-trained warriors increase the likelihood of success, then that might entail the end of conflict, and enable refugees to return to their homes (as is currently the case with the Karen in Thailand). Was this the reason for the government's sympathy toward the freedom fighters? Sisson and Rose (1990) argue that the arms provided by the Indian government to the freedom fighters were of low quality, even obsolete, which shows that India's support was more symbolic than strategic. Was the Indian government actually concerned about militarization?

It is difficult to make a case either way here, because the topic of militarization was not debated in the Indian Parliament during this period. Some newspapers reported on militarization (e.g., the *Far Eastern Economic Review*, cited above), but did not reveal the government's negative attitude toward militarization. Thus, although militarization in a general sense can create aggressive tendencies, in this particular case it does not seem to have done so.

Shared Bangali ethnicity

Shared ethnic ties were important as well. Despite the heavy toll that refugees imposed on the economy, thirty out of the fifty respondents to the India Survey stated that they were sympathetic to the cause at the time, and that over time their feelings either remained unchanged (five respondents) or they became more sympathetic (twenty-five). Of the thirty sympathetic respondents, fourteen had Bangali friends from East Bengal living with them which can explain the root of their sympathy. All fifty respondents said that they supported the formation of Bangladesh as a new country.

One respondent, who was aged fifteen at the time, said:

> I, of course, was too young in 1971. All I remember are the blackouts in the evenings; our windows were painted up so that light didn't spill out and we would hear fighter planes droning overhead! I also remember that we gave part of our rations [India operated a ration card system whereby individuals received subsidized commodities from the state] to the refugees from East Pakistan. It was not mandatory but most families we knew gave it to fellow Bengalis. So, that was the feeling—there was a pride in [Sheikh] Mujib, and a great feeling prevailed in West Bengal that the nation-state of India under Indira Gandhi was helping fellow Bengalis. The story goes that Madam Gandhi asked Field Marshal Maneckshaw to send only Bengali [Indian] pilots to the war in the first raid because she could sense the overwhelming Bengali pride in West Bengal!
> (Dhaka, August 14, 2010)

In addition, the Indian states were concerned about the possible collusion of the Communist Party (CPM) and Naxalites (CPML) in West Bengal with "leftists" in East Pakistan (namely the Purbo Bangla Communist Party or the East Bengal Communist Party), who together had the ability to undermine the Central Government in India. West Bengal had already undergone violence and unrest owing to Maoist insurgencies in 1965; periods of "President's Rule" (direct federal control) were imposed. If the East Pakistani elements joined the local forces, it would be a catastrophe from India's point of view (Stern 2001; Sisson and Rose 1990; Marwah 1979). It is unclear how valid such concerns were, however, because the communist elements were anti-India as well as anti-Bangladesh (and in fact anti-Establishment generally) and labeled the War of Independence as bourgeois, as attested by many of the respondents to the Bangladesh Survey. The Maoist orientation of the communist parties made them pro-Pakistan through transitivity: Maoists were pro-China, China was pro-Pakistan, and hence the Maoists were also pro-Pakistan, and in effect anti-liberation and anti-revolution. Although shared ethnicity explains the support that Bangladeshis received from fellow Bangalis in India, it does not explain why India intervened militarily.

Irredentism

Some of the respondents to the India Survey mentioned that Indira Gandhi may have feared moves toward irredentism and thus intervened to prevent that. India referred to East Pakistan as East Bengal—its original name before Bengal was divided into two with the partition of India—and many outsiders wondered whether using the former name bore any relation to West Bengal's separatist interests. According to one respondent, the main reason for India's intervention may have been "the humanitarian and justice angle," but "it is said Madam Gandhi preempted the unification of Bengal, which meant the division of India, and thus stepped into the war in order to gain greater control."

India's former Minister of Foreign Affairs Sardar Swaran Singh visited the United States in June 1971, when he spoke at the National Press Club in Washington, DC, and addressed questions of irredentism and the reasons for which India referred to East Pakistan as East Bengal. He argued that the people of West Bengal are Indians—the implication being that they are proud Indians and would always choose their Indian national identity over Bangali identity.

> The use of this expression does not mean that there is any risk of West Bengal, which is a state of the Indian Union, at any time thinking of joining East Bengal, even if it becomes independent. They know the value of being equal partners in this great country of ours, India, where they have played a significant role in the political field, in the social and economic field; and thus I do not realize that there is ever any risk of people of West Bengal, constituent state of India, ever thinking of opting out of India, whatever is the future of East Pakistan.
>
> (Singh 1999: 686)

That the government had to respond to claims of irredentism indicates that it may have had some concerns. The insurgencies of the 1960s had alienated West Bengal from the Central Government to a certain degree. Popular Bengla movies of the time in West Bengal also mentioned "waiting for the day when Bengal is united," and thus failed to assuage concerns about loyalty.

An interesting element is how West Bengal supported the war with a similar degree of fervor to that of India's independence struggle in the 1930s, and employed the same types of rhetoric about oppression and self-determination. For example, patriotic songs about the spirit of Bengal were revived and played on the radio with the aim of creating unity and inspiring soldiers. "In many ways," said one India Survey respondent, "this was our war, since it was a war about Bangla and its survival."

However, it is difficult to separate such sentiments from the bond of shared ethnicity. While there is much to suggest that West Bangalis shared many ideological principles with their East Bangali brethren, the political and military apparatus did not exist to enable any form of movement to support irredentism. Such talk may have had popular value, but there were no efforts to turn talk into reality.

Electoral mandate

Indira Gandhi won the March 1971 national election largely owing to her *Garibi Hatao* ("End Poverty") election campaign. With refugees placing a strain on already limited resources, it was quite clear that Gandhi would not be able to adhere to her mandate. Although locals in West Bengal were largely sympathetic toward refugees owing to ethnic ties and would overlook this failure, locals in areas such as Assam and Tripura became disgruntled. The introduction of new ration cards for refugees had generated inflationary pressures, raising the prices of basic food items and stirring up grievances among locals.

Partly for reelection purposes, Gandhi had to ensure that the refugees would not impose a long-term problem (N. Sengupta 2007). It is unclear whether or not this was a major issue, however. The refugee influx was an external shock that could not be attributed to Gandhi or the Congress Party. Would the voting public not recognize the difference between deliberate and inadvertent breaking of promises?

India-Pakistan power play or Indian hegemony?

India maintained that during the war, the international community and of course Pakistan had tried to frame the refugee issue as an India-Pakistan issue or as an internal problem of Pakistan, thereby neglecting long-term refugee concerns that brought life in West Bengal and other border areas to a standstill. As schools and universities were closed in order to house refugees, inflationary pressures crept in.

Strategically, if Pakistan could convince the world—and its population in West Pakistan—that the crisis was a product of India-Pakistan rivalry and not of Pakistan's military repression of its population in the east, it could escape international (and domestic) rebuke. Especially given that Pakistan's sense of national unity was based on anti-India sentiments, claiming that rebels in East Pakistan were Indian pawns provided military and political mileage as well as international and domestic support.

In Gandhi's May 24, 1971 speech to the Lok Sabha (lower house of Parliament), she stated that it was "mischievous to suggest that India has had anything to do with what happened in Bangladesh. This is an insult to the aspirations and spontaneous sacrifices of the people of Bangladesh, and a calculated attempt by the rulers of Pakistan to make India a scapegoat for their own misdeeds. It is also a crude attempt to deceive the world community." (Singh 1999: 672)

Samar Sen, India's permanent representative to the UN, criticized the UN for allowing perceptions of India-Pakistan rivalry to pervade the international community without understanding the fundamental facts. In a speech at the UN on May 11, 1971 he said,

> There was a great hue and cry to internationalize the problem: diplomatic moves, various moves in the United Nations through these proposals for observers, and this, that, and the other—all designed to make it into an Indo-Pakistan dispute. Once it turned into an Indo-Pakistan dispute, people will forget what the Pakistan Army is doing in East Pakistan. They can go on burning their villages, raping their women and so on. People will then forget and say that it is an Indo-Pakistan dispute. It is extraordinary, therefore, to find that today, when pressure for action is so great in some quarters, this background is forgotten.
>
> (Singh 1999: 682)

It was in India's interest to play down the rivalry factor and focus more on the humanitarian issues involved. After all, why should India not capitalize on Pakistan's weakness and strike when victory was almost assured, particularly when it had a legitimate humanitarian reason to do so? One difficulty in assessing the relevance of India-Pakistan rivalry is the lack of evidence to support either story. Even if dividing Pakistan was on the agenda, this was never expressed publicly. That India did not discuss the Pakistan factor may indicate strategic behavior, i.e., choosing to focus on the humanitarian plight of refugees because that would be more popular. However, a war with Pakistan would probably be domestically popular. Why sould such concerns not be made public? Perhaps the question is one of the long-term versus the short-term outcome. While in the immediate term it was important to focus on the pressing matter of the refugees, India may have realized that the long-term effect of resolving a short-term problem through intervention would be promising in terms of winning regional dominance.

The international community's limited concern

During parliamentary discussions about the effect of the refugees on India's economy, a recurring theme was frustration that India alone had to carry the burden. The prime minister not only argued that this was an international crisis, but also sent emissaries abroad to garner support for Bangladesh. Gandhi felt that the international community should pressure the Pakistani government to end the genocide. The generation of refugees, further, turned the crisis into an international event, one that therefore might justify some kind of international intervention.

Gandhi argued that "the Great Powers [had] a special responsibility," and were in a position to bring about long-lasting peace in the Indian sub-continent purely through rhetoric. Why did the world take such a long time to rebuke Pakistan? Interestingly, there was no mention of Cold War politics, although these did seem to constrain world response. The United States, for example, was preoccupied with communism and sought to use Pakistan to reach out to China in order to stem it. Human rights violations and genocides did not seem to matter. However, many respondents to the India and Bangladesh surveys wondered why the US public cared so little about genocide in Bangladesh while protesting the Vietnam War for essentially the same kinds of issues.

On May 24, 1971, while addressing the Lok Sabha, Indira Gandhi emphatically stated,

> The problems which confront us are not confined to Assam, Meghalaya, Tripura, and West Bengal. They are national problems. Indeed, the basic problem is an international one. We have sought to awaken the conscience of the world through our representatives abroad and the representatives of foreign Governments in India. We have appealed to the United Nations. However, I must share with the House our disappointment at the unconscionably long time which the world is taking to react to this stark tragedy.
>
> (Singh 1999: 672)

There was considerable international pressure on Pakistan to resolve the issues, although its focus was more on refugees than on the legitimacy of the elected government. The UN Secretary-General U Thant condemned Pakistani action in East Pakistan and requested the international community to assist India in its efforts to provide refuge to those fleeing the conflict. Thant's message seemed to signify that the international community was aware of the situation and even willing to help the refugee community. However, Cold War politics got in the way. In an appeal dated May 19, 1971, Thant said,

> The international community has been seriously concerned at the plight of the sizable and continuing influx of refugees ... from East Pakistan

into adjacent states of India. I fully share this concern. Mindful that one of the purposes of the United Nations is "to achieve international co-operation in solving international problems of a humanitarian character," I am convinced that the United Nations and its family of Organizations have an important role to play in alleviating the serious hardship and suffering which these refugees are undergoing.

(Singh 1999: 675)

Thant instructed UNHCR to send a three-man team to judge the situation on the ground, but stalemate ensued as the major powers chose to remain "neutral." The United States did not want to antagonize Pakistan for fear of "losing" China; the Soviet Union did not want to get embroiled in another conflict; China, having fought a war with India in 1962, was not willing to get involved either. Given the inaction of the major powers India decided to mobilize its embassies.

Speaking at the National Press Club in Washington, DC, in June 1971, Sardar Swaran Singh argued that the mere disapproval of the United States could "have a powerful impact upon the military rulers [and] will be a strong deterrent against the continued military action by the perpetrators."

Following her ambassadors' failure to influence world leaders, Gandhi embarked on a world tour. She held talks with President Nixon in Washington, DC, and gave speeches in several European cities. During every visit, she made it clear that India was running out of resources to support the refugees and that some form of international action would be required. Initially, India demanded only strong words from the international community, but as time progressed, the country's stance hardened and became more agressive. While in Germany in November 1971, Gandhi voiced her exasperation and frustration with the ongoing situation, and deplored the fact that the world (mainly the United States) chose to ignore the refugees' plight and the circumstances that had rendered them homeless. India's geographic location bordering East Pakistan to the east, north, and west, meant that the country faced imported problems alone. Gandhi declared,

I very authoritatively say that I will not tolerate these refugees living in India. I am very definite, and so is our entire country. We have borne a very big burden with hardly any help from outside, and when we drew the attention of the UN, we were given the answer: "It is an internal problem of Pakistan. We cannot interfere in it." There are nearly 10 million people and the UN just says "we are very sorry, we do not mind if millions of people have been killed in Pakistan it is an internal matter of Pakistan."

(Singh 1999: 283)

If one traces the changes in rhetoric used at home and abroad these reveal the way that India's disposition altered in terms of what a durable solution to the refugee problem might be. The majority of India's relief operations were planned to last six months. Prior to India's intervention in December 1971, India had asked the UN and the United States to take collective action to end the refugee influx, but made it clear that in the absence of such action, it would be forced to intervene militarily. As such, this demonstrated that India had been willing to show restraint up until this point.

Some criticism was expressed that India did not allow UNHCR to operate fully in the camps. However, India's concern was that repatriating the refugees while conditions remained unchanged in their homeland would not help the situation. In other words, returning the refugees was tantamount to treating only the symptoms of the problem. India sought UN support both to protect the refugees and to find a long-term solution.

The international community's lack of support had multiple effects. First, it made India realize that it was the sole bearer of the refugee burden. Second, it signaled to India that any action India undertook would probably have little consequence because of international complacency. Third, it reflected the atmosphere of the time: a greater focus on Cold War issues rather than on geopolitical or humanitarian issues in regions of little strategic importance. All of these factors combined to give India the strength to pursue its foreign policy based primarily on domestic policy, without fearing international reprimand.

Refugee concerns: an estimate of the refugee burden

Number of refugees

The sheer magnitude of the refugees' effect on the Indian economy was overwhelming. Perhaps because India was more accessible to journalists than East Pakistan, much of the international media coverage regarding the crisis in 1971 focused on the refugees. Figure 6.1 shows the influx of refugees into India during the nine-month period beginning in April 1971. In the first month following Bangladesh's declaration of independence on March 26, 1971 three million refugees entered India. By June, however, the monthly influx had fallen to less than one million a month, and it then decreased rapidly to 166,000 in December 1971 when the war ended. Table 6.1 shows the number of camps in each region and the population of refugees both inside and outside the refugee camps. Undoubtedly, these numbers are large, but to put this into perspective, Table 6.2 shows the proportion of refugees relative to the population of the region.

It is worth noting that the refugee population in Tripura was almost as large as the local population (see Table 6.2). Not surprisingly, locals in this region were antagonistic toward the new arrivals. According to a report in the *Far Eastern Economic Review* on September 2, 1971, Tripura's relief secretary expressed concerns over the long-term consequences of hosting such a large number of refugees, indicating that animosity among locals would be likely due to perceptions of, as well as real, competition.

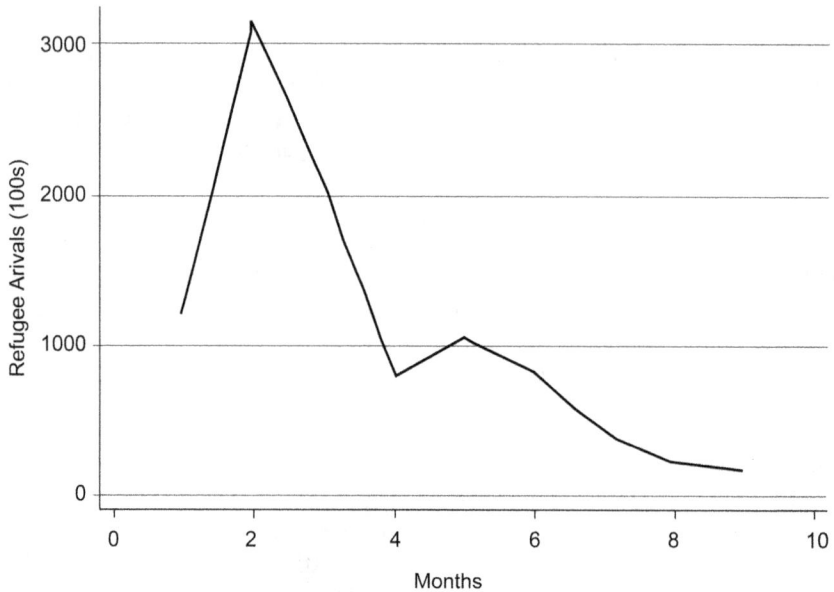

Figure 6.1 Refugee influx into India during the nine-month period from April to December 1971

Table 6.1 Refugees in and out of camps as at December 15, 1971

State	No. of camps	In camps	Outside camps	Total
West Bengal	492	4,849,786	2,386,130	7,235,916
Tripura	276	834,098	64,713	1,381,649
Meghalaya	17	591,520	76,466	667,986
Assam	28	255,642	91,913	347,555
Bihar	8	36,732	n/a	36,732
Madhya Pradesh	3	219,298	n/a	219,298
Uttar Pradesh	1	10,169	n/a	10,169
Total	825	6,797,245	3,102,060	9,899,299

Table 6.2 Influx of refugees relative to local population

State	Refugees	Local population	Ratio
Assam	313	14,952	0.02
Bihar	983	56,383	0.017
Tripura	1,416	1,557	0.90
West Bengal	7,493	44,440	0.16

Our local population is friendly because we have assured them the refugees are only here for six months. This is tribal country. Local people ... are very jealous of their land rights. If they think these people are here permanently, we may have serious trouble. Locals are already complaining because prices have gone up since the refugees have been forced to buy in the open market after the ration cut.

(Far Eastern Economic Review 1971)

Finances

India allocated Rs. 2.6 billion for refugees, but their estimated need was Rs. 4.2 billion, according to the statement given by India's Rehabilitation Secretary, Shri G. S. Kahlon, at the 22nd session of the executive committee of UNHCR held in Geneva on October 5, 1971.[2] In addition to listing the various costs associated with hosting refugees, he stated that the burden was too severe for India to bear alone and urged the international community to help.

The extremely heavy expenditure involved in providing relief assistance to these refugees, whose number is mounting every day, is causing a severe financial strain on India's economy. The Government of India has, therefore, urged the United Nations and Foreign Governments, through Indian Missions abroad, to share the responsibility in tackling this vast refugee problem which should be the concern of the International Community.

(Singh 1999: 92)

According to newspaper sources, a ration card was issued to all refugees that granted them rice, *dal* (lentils), and vegetables. A stipend was given too, but that shrank from Rs. 15 in April to Rs. 1 in October, indicating a considerable drop in how much could be done for the refugees.

During this nine-month period there were significant discussions within the Rajya Sabha (upper house of Parliament) and the Lok Sabha, regarding the costs associated with hosting refugees. India's representatives abroad also tried to persuade UNHCR and other international bodies to help ease the burden. The general feeling seemed to be that India, despite its best efforts, was being overwhelmed by the cost. Early on in the crisis, Indira Gandhi spoke of shortages of living space and essentials; many schools and universities became designated refugee camps. Addressing the Lok Sabha on May 24, 1971 Gandhi said that

every available building, including schools and training institutions, has been requisitioned. Thousands of tents have been pitched and temporary shelters are being constructed as quickly as possible in the 335 camps which have been established so far. In spite of our best efforts we have not been able to provide shelter to all those who have come across, and many are still in the open. The district authorities are under severe strain. Before they can cope with those who are already here, 60,000 more are coming across every day. Medical facilities in all our border States have been stretched to breaking point.

(Singh 1999: 672)

On June 15, 1971, Gandhi again addressed the Rajya Sabha. She pointed out that no developed country in the world had so far had to face such a situation, and yet the world expected impoverished India to carry the burden alone.

When any country has to face a large influx—not an influx over a long period, but a sudden influx within a few weeks, of nearly six million people—it is not a joke; it is not a small thing. I would like to know from honorable members: do they know of any country in the world which has faced even one-tenth of this situation before? It is very easy to sit in this House and just criticize and criticize. If even ten thousand refugees arrive in any European country, the whole Continent of Europe will be afire with all the newspapers, the Governments; and everybody will be aroused. We are trying to deal with nearly six million human beings who have fled from a region of terror, who have come wounded, with disease, with illness, hunger, and exhaustion. In this country we have a shortage of practically everything which [refugees] need. We have a shortage of tarpaulins; we have a shortage of corrugated iron sheets; we have a shortage of every possible thing you can think of. We have tried to round these items from every part of the country; we are rushing them to the camps. But no matter what we do—I am sorry to say—we cannot keep [supporting the] refugees.

(Singh 1999: 683)

Despite the support of local Indians, especially in West Bengal, Gandhi's words reflect the desperation experienced at national level: it was no longer about the willingness, but the capacity to support such a large group.

In his speech to the UN Security Council on May 17, 1971, Samar Sen emphasized India's inability to sustain the refugee burden and deplored the international community's refusal to acknowledge the severity of the situation in East Pakistan. He also averred that India could no longer "tolerate" the situation (Singh 1999). It is difficult to assess whether his words were intended to convey a threat or an expression of frustration. Perhaps India's state of development did not make its implicit threats of aggression very credible. Even if other factors played a contributing role, such as the India-Pakistan rivalry, the sudden and immediate cost that India experienced cannot be overlooked.

An evaluation of these factors makes one thing certain: the need to end the conflict on India's eastern border. Although many geopolitical and strategic reasons may have helped to enlist domestic support for intervention, the immediate burden imposed by the refugees was overwhelming in terms of the numbers and finance involved. As Minister of Foreign Affairs Singh stated during his visit to the US in 1971, "there are other ways of enforcing [action without] declaring war. And, I hope we will not be compelled to resort to those other means, which perhaps you cannot expect me to spell out at this stage" (Singh 1999: 686).

Even in June 1971 India hoped that international pressure would bring an end to Pakistan's military regime and force it to accept the election results. It also becomes clear that by May/June 1971, India's resources were stretched thin, overwhelmed by the mass of refugees entering the country. India responded by trying to mobilize the international community to take some form of action. When diplomatic talks failed, Prime Minister Gandhi herself embarked on a world tour to garner support. She and her ministers were adamant that India would be unable to support the refugees for longer than six months, but could not be specific about what would happen when that period was over. Perhaps India's intervention is not so surprising after all.

Conclusion

In the short term, intervention for India meant refugee repatriation; in the long term, it meant a divided Pakistan and regional dominance. While the long-term incentives for a country such as India seeking a dominant position may be ever present, they have little power to explain the timing of this intervention. The refugee problem provides the answer. Having found that the international community would remain deaf to its calls for help, India utilized a cost-benefit analysis based purely on its national interests (refugees, costs, inflation, living space), realizing that at the systemic level there were gains to be had without the costs as an externality (regional dominance). In this light, intervention was certainly India's best response to the crisis.

Critics would probably argue that it was India's rivalry with Pakistan that brought India to war or that Pakistan's incursion on India's western border (Kashmir) "provoked" India's action on the eastern border. In response, I would point out that India and Pakistan had engaged in a series of border disputes over Kashmir since 1947. India could have used its ethnic ties to East Pakistan to "destabilize" Pakistan during those times as well. Why did India wait until 1971 to use East Pakistan/East Bengal as leverage? My argument is that the refugees created a unique situation that required Indian action in order to end the crisis and ease the burden on India's economy. The refugees were more than a pretext for war because the 10-million-person burden they imposed had dire consequences for the average Indian living near camp areas. Its rivalry with Pakistan may have been a contributing factor, but it was not the primary reason why India intervened in Bangladesh's War of Independence.

During the last forty years, India has developed dramatically in both economic and military terms, especially relative to its neighbors, most notably

Pakistan. Did Pakistan's division aid that process? If the answer is a definitive "yes," then India's action in 1971 could be justified along such lines, at least in retrospect. However, Pakistan has maintained that East Pakistan did not add much to its economy, as a result of which its secession did not have much impact. In contrast, one can argue that the loss of East Pakistan meant the loss of cultural and ethnic diversity, the loss of a moderate voice in an Islamic state, and the loss of democratic principles which eventually stunted Pakistan's rise, despite reaching nuclear parity with India. Moreover, in 1971 India signaled to the world that it would not sit idle when its national interests were at stake. Even though India's action at the time was based on the state of the economy as impacted by refugees, its longer-term effect has been to establish India as a credible regional power. Thus the only humanitarian intervention in the short history of independent South Asian nations had elements of Waltzian neorealism.

Notes

1 There were many refugees in Thailand as well, but Thailand did not intervene. Part of the reason that Vietnam intervened and Thailand did not may be that the refugees in Thailand were better looked after by international NGOs and the UN. Refugees in Vietnam were less privileged and had little access to international NGOs or the UN. So, while Thailand benefited monetarily from hosting refugees, Vietnam did not. Thailand did, however, use low-scale violence to force repatriation.
2 In 1971 US $1 was equivalent to approximately 7.50 Indian rupees. The rupee was pegged to the gold standard until December 1971.

7 Conclusion

Almost every family in South Asia has a refugee story to tell. Many people share a sense of belonging somewhere else, even though their story about migration may go back many generations. "We are a nation of refugees—we have all been refugees at one time or another in Iran, in Pakistan, or somewhere else," an Afghan man told me. "I'm Indian, but I really feel like I'm a refugee—I feel like an outsider everywhere," an Indian Bangali man stated. In this book I have endeavored to bring together several dimensions of the state of being a refugee and statelessness. In particular, I have sought to explain that "refugee" in the South Asian context is a loose term that applies to anyone who does not "belong." And the state decides who belongs.

This book assembles a diverse set of literature with a view to considering refugees' participation in political activities. There exists very little literature on protests among refugees; what does exist examines protests in the context of militarization. As a result, refugees' political activities are lumped together as "refugee-related violence," which encompasses everything from protests, sit-ins, and demonstrations to riots and militarization (Lischer 2005). To move away from this aggregation, I relied on a modified version of the contentious-politics literature in order to analyze protests, while using the "refugee-warrior" literature to stimulate the discussion on militarization. In distinguishing between protests and militarization, I have attempted to demonstrate that the motives and the mechanisms for each are different. In addition, I have endeavored to decriminalize protests among refugees and to portray militarization geared at national self-determination as legitimate.

There are two somewhat contradictory parts to the argument that I have put forward here. On the one hand, I argue that refugees have agency, that they are not voiceless victims in need of perpetual help; on the other hand, I argue that militancy among refugees stems from the way in which they are manipulated by states, which take advantage of their despair. If refugees are susceptible to manipulation, is their voice not limited, at least to a certain degree?

What is crucial to understand in the South Asian context is the on-the-ground reality of abject poverty—the fact that what most refugees have in common is a lack of access to basic material needs. This is important because the motivation to better their material conditions prompts refugees to act in the manner they do, whether in the form of protesting for rights within the existing framework or in indirect ways, such as becoming tools for manipulation. Hence, when refugees are "coerced" by states to act in certain ways, they do in fact exercise their voice—but their judgment is clouded by their often desperate conditions. Pragmatically, then, refugees have agency until that moment of desperation. At the same time, there are instances when "manipulation" serves refugees' political objectives, as demonstrated by the support for the Mukti Bahini (see Chapter 6), for example. In such situations, refugees are not manipulated because they are desperate or weak; refugees allow themselves to be manipulated because it bolsters their strength and gives them access and privileges that the state would otherwise deny them.

The refugees' stories in Chapter 2 offer some traction on this question. Clearly, there is a difference between a wealthy refugee and a poor one; between an encamped refugee and one who is able to move about freely; a refugee with or without an identity card; a refugee who is patronized by the state and one who isn't. It all boils down to class. It is class that foretells refugee experiences. It is class that dictates the point at which refugees lose their voices and become desperate pawns. I started with the refugees' stories to remind myself and the reader that we are talking about *people* when we use judgment-laden words like "refugee warriors" and "war entrepreneurs," when we talk about how refugees contribute to the spread of regional conflict.

What I hope has become clear over the course of the book is the fluid nature of identity, much of which has been influenced by population movements. There is shared heritage, language, and culture all across South Asia; yet, state-based politics have attempted to create monocultures by denying shared identities and attempting to create a "self" at the expense of artificially created "others," differences that over time became real. The Ghoti–Bangal divide is just one such example.

"The only solution to statelessness is for stateless people to acquire a nationality," states the UNHCR's *Global Report* (UNHCR 2011). At this juncture we need to consider whether there are solutions to refugee crises that rely on a single state—more specifically, the receiving state. International organizations such as UNHCR claim that refugees are the responsibility of the receiving state, but what does that mean? In the context of South Asia, such humanitarian organizations tell a consistently patronizing tale: given that India, Bangladesh, and Pakistan are not signatories to the Refugee Convention or its Protocol, these states go above and beyond their duties and responsibilities to protect refugees. Such patronization absolves these states of their responsibilities at a time when international organizations prescribe state-based solutions.

We need to be mindful that the system has failed: the refugee crises in South Asia are protracted ones that needed resolution thirty years ago. There are generations of refugees and refugee children who have grown up without belonging, without a home, for whom struggle—whether for survival or by taking up arms—has been the only way of life. To a certain degree, all three states have cited refugees as a source of national insecurity and criminalization. Yet there has been little effort to end such crises once and for all. Thus, we need to pause and focus on a more comprehensive, more credible solution. It will have to begin with the recognition that India, Bangladesh, and Pakistan cannot do much as sole actors—not because they do not have resources, but because they have vested interests, if not a direct conflict of interest.

As I have argued, the state has an interest in allowing for protraction. Refugees are easy to manipulate because they are desperate, and can be used as a scapegoat because they have little recourse to justice and self-defense, both of which can be employed by the state for nationalistic goals, whether in terms of fostering unity in the face of "infiltrators" or striving for regional dominance by using refugees as pawns. In such a scenario, then, is there any hope that receiving states will be credible protectors of refugees?

At a very basic level, the analysis presented in this book calls for a shift in understanding of refugee politics toward a more "stateless" approach. The basis of many of the present refugee issues is the issue of statelessness, where people are denied citizenship by a state explicitly or implicitly. Rabindranath Tagore, in an essay entitled "Nationalism in India," wrote,

> The most important fact of the present age is that all the different races of men have come close together. ... The problem is whether the different groups of peoples shall go on fighting with one another or find out some true basis of reconciliation and mutual help; whether it will be interminable competition or cooperation. I have no hesitation in saying that those who are gifted with moral power of love and vision of spiritual unity, who have the least feeling of enmity against aliens, and the sympathetic insight to place themselves in the position of others, will be the fittest to take their permanent place in the age that is lying before us, and those who are constantly developing their instincts for fight and intolerance of aliens will be eliminated. For this is the problem before us, and we have to prove our humanity by solving it through the help of our higher nature. ... During the evolution of the Nation the moral culture of brotherhood was limited by geographical boundaries, because at that time those boundaries were true. Now they have become imaginary lines of tradition divested of the qualities of real obstacles. So the time has come when man's moral nature must deal with this great fact with all seriousness of perish.
>
> (1917)

The same issues exist today. Almost 100 years later, I sing a similar tune: at the core of any permanent change in the protection of refugees on the part of the receiving state is the need to shed nationalistic xenophobia. The identification of "others" in the South Asian context is particularly farcical given that, as a consequence of shared history, physically everyone looks like one another, especially in border areas. Likewise, many languages and dialects are spoken across borders. Nationalists will argue that Urdu and Hindi are vastly different languages, or that the version of Bangla spoken in West Bengal and Bangladesh are too different to be considered the same, but the fact remains that despite slight variations in "culture," the people of India, Bangladesh, and Pakistan are closer than they would like to believe. Thus, when each state treats refugees/people from the other states with hostility, it is purely a function of state-sponsored propaganda.

It is no easy task, however, to bring about a sea change in how people think about "outsiders," as the past 100 years of South Asian history have shown. The constructivist notion of changing or recreating identities in a manner that ensures that a "rise" in one identity is not at the expense of others is, perhaps, the way forward; it is when "imagined communities" become rigid that the seeds of xenophobia begin to germinate (Anderson 1983). Any change in people's perceptions needs to begin with a refashioning of national politics and policies to avoid using the "foreigner threat" as a source of national unity.

The constructivist idea of shaping identities is also relevant at a broader level if we think of the role that norms and international law can have in shaping state responses to refugees. Citizenship, a dominant factor in protracted crises not only in South Asia but around the world, ought to be a universal human right. No state should have the power to declare some of its population "noncitizens" or "foreigners." There is a need for a globally accepted, objective charter that lays out the factors for determining citizenship to prevent states from taking away citizenship arbitrarily. This means relying on international organizations and having faith that they will act independently and neutrally, without being influenced by patrons and donors. This, too, is no easy task, as concerns over the credibility of international institutions show (Stiglitz 2001; Stone 2004).

What is a "stateless" approach? Such an approach takes as its premise that state-based solutions have failed. The practical reality is that the receiving state is not always best positioned to address and resolve refugee issues, especially in cases where refugee influxes are sudden and from bordering states. It is not only vested interests that delegitimize the role of the state; the state has all kinds of concerns—economic, security, etc.—which prevent it from being a pro-refugee advocate. As this book has demonstrated, the receiving state can perceive refugees in the light of multiple threats, imagined or real, that can prevent it from championing the rights of refugees in good faith. Thus, even though the current international regime is a proponent of states taking responsibility for refugees, this approach is actually counterproductive.

Once we recognize this critical limitation on the part of the state, the question is: what is a pro-refugee solution? We need to stop thinking of refugees as "lesser people" and thereby deserving of their fate. This is no easy task.

We need to ask why the state can take away or impede basic human rights legitimately. This recognition can help us to realize that nationalism is a tool for state propaganda. I have argued here that refugee manipulation serves nationalistic purposes. However, the issue at hand is more severe because the nature of propaganda is such that citizens get brainwashed into believing what the state churns out; every citizen can become an agent of the state, upholding its notion of nationalism. Of course, this is an exaggeration, but it does not understate the potential impact of state propaganda in its most extreme form. This is problematic because it turns citizens into oppressors of refugee groups (and of other minority groups and foreigners).

There is a need for state-level cooperation as well: the receiving state, the sending state, and international organizations need to discuss crises in good faith with resolution as an end goal. Why cannot the Rohingya continue to live in Rakhine in Myanmar? Would it really hurt Bangladesh so much if a few hundred thousand people joined its population of 150 million? Does India really need to encamp 200,000 "illegal Bangladeshis" who have set up home in India? How ironic is it that borders designed to protect people not only created unthinkable violence during the Partition years but continue to hurt people today? Have we learned nothing from the horror of Partition? Why do we continue to allow borders to divide and dehumanize people? In the long term, the solution to refugee crises and protracted refugee camps lies in recognizing the right to movement across borders.

To summarize, then, the solution involves four demands:

1 States should avoid creating nationalist propaganda that relies on anti-neighbor sentiments.
2 States should actively denounce racism and xenophobia.
3 States should not have the authority to decide arbitrarily that certain groups do not belong to the state—an independent, nonpartisan international organization needs to create some standard procedures for determining the citizenship of stateless people.
4 As a long-term goal, states need to move toward an international regime whereby individuals can freely move from one country to another. In South Asia, SAARC can be the regional body that facilitates the transition to free mobility.

I conclude by reverting to stories—stories that highlight the inadequacies of this book in giving a complete account of the many intricacies involved in refugees' daily lives, intricacies that combine to create ground realities that are unique and even unimaginable to those who never interact with refugees; stories of individuals who have exercised agency against all odds in a way that is unimaginable for non-refugees; stories that I hope will make us think twice before we label human beings.

• There is an Afghan woman who is actually from Bangladesh. She was orphaned as a child, sold by her aunt, trafficked to India, sold as a sex slave to a Pakistani, and sent to an Afghan refugee camp in Peshawar, where an Afghan refugee fell in love with her and they decided to make a life together. Today she is an "Afghan," but her roots are all over the subcontinent.

- There are two Sikh Afghan brothers who have been living in Delhi for decades. They can be found at the Foreigner Regional Registration Office every year renewing their visas. Most of us think of Afghans only as Muslims, but these men are Sikhs and they are afraid to go back to Afghanistan.
- There is a Nepali hairdresser, a woman who can pass as someone from the northeast, in Gurgaon, Haryana. She says she faces no problems living there by herself, in a place where she is visibly different from locals and that is well-known for bigotry, where even people from the northeast are not safe.
- There is a girl whose grandparents migrated from East Bengal to West Bengal during Partition. She herself was born in India, but her non-Bangali friends call her "Bangladeshi"—even though she has never been to Bangladesh.
- There is a young man who, feeling "homeless" in West Bengal because his parents were from the East, went to live in Bangladesh but could not find "home."
- There is a Chin refugee who went to Delhi via Mizoram, where she was raped by a local policeman. She has a three-year old daughter who is a daily reminder of that rape. She now works at a textile factory in Uttamnagar.
- There is a taxi driver in Delhi who spoke of the riches of his ancestral home in Pakistan. Those stories keep his spirits high.
- There is a third-generation Muhajir who proudly claims that he is Pakistani and not a Muhajir, at a time when most Pakistanis identify themselves with one of four (or five) ethnic groups—Punjabi, Pashtun, Balochi, or Sindhi (and Muhajir).
- There are some border guards along the Bangladesh-Myanmar border who took pity on the Rohingya and looked away to facilitate their entry into Bangladesh after the borders were closed down.
- There is a *dalal* who helps refugees to obtain passports and assists their migration in the direst of conditions. He has helped many to go from one country to another.

These stories cannot be incorporated into a single, consistent story about refugee behavior. They are not in keeping with theoretical constructs to explain "the conditions under which refugees protest or engage in militarization" (see Chapter 3 and Chapter 4). They depict the survival skills of ordinary people who take great risks to protect their families, the free will of people as they vote with their feet. Some of these stories also reflect acts of kindness that are technically illegal, but provide some hope for a future when borders will not be used as a tool to discriminate, humiliate, and kill.

Appendix 1
Data on protests and militarization

Much of the work on camp security, safety, and refugees' participation in political activities is based on case studies (Loescher 1989; Lischer 2003; etc.). While such works are interesting and insightful, it is difficult to gauge the degree to which the findings are comparable, given the different definitions of security, safety, and militarization used in various studies. Thus it is hard to discuss patterns that may explain certain tendencies among refugees— toward protesting, for example. The various definitions and portrayals of militarization make it challenging to distinguish between degrees of political participation, peaceful or otherwise. It was this problem that led me to begin the data collection process that I used in Chapter 2 and Chapter 3.

I collected the data from the country pages for India, Pakistan, and Bangladesh on the UNHCR website (www.unhcr.org) as well as from the UNHCR Global Reports. I accessed newspaper sources for the three countries via BBC Monitoring,[1] a service that since 2006 has collected news from all local (vernacular) news sources in a given country. For news sources prior to 2006, I used the following newspapers' archives: the *Hindu* in India, the *Dawn* in Pakistan, the *Daily Star*[2] and *Bangladesh Observer*[3] in Bangladesh.

There are three problems with this approach, in addition to those commonly encountered with media-generated data. First, I could only gather aggregate data at group level (as opposed to camp-level data). Second, given the limited exposure that refugees get in the media, I could only include activities that the local media deemed to be "newsworthy," which rarely occurs more than once a year; thus, I had to code the variables on an annual basis. Even though an incident, whatever it may be, may last just a few weeks rather than an entire year, the annual structure of the data makes it appear as though the incident lasted all year. The problem that stems from this structure is that many actions may appear to occur simultaneously, although they may be sequential. Third, the data and all information included here pertain to refugees who were registered either by the receiving state or by UNHCR.

From the time of independence (1947 for India and Pakistan; 1971 for Bangladesh) a total of ten refugee groups have lived in the three countries for a minimum of one year (Bangalis in India) to a maximum of forty years (Biharis in Bangladesh). The resulting dataset consists of 155 group-years from 1947 to 2011.

The coding process of some of the key variables is as follows.

Separatism: For all refugee groups under consideration, I checked to see whether the newspaper sources identified the groups as having tendencies toward self-determination, and if so, what the time frame was. For example, during the initial period in the 1980s when the Tamils from Sri Lanka were taking refuge in India, the media portrayed them as having separatist tendencies; India was accused of supporting and providing training to Tamil rebels. However, over time, the "cause of independence" died down considerably; from 1994 onward, some Tamils were repatriated voluntarily. India still hosts about 80,000 refugees from Sri Lanka (as at 2012), and there is little talk of a separate Tamil state. The LTTE, the group that headed the Tamil separatist movement, evolved into more of a terrorist group that relied on suicide bombing as a weapon, rather than being an organization for freedom fighters.

Expected length of stay: For this variable, I assessed the media's perception of how long the refugees would stay in the host country. When refugees first arrive in a host country, the media usually provide a sense of how long they are expected to stay, depending on the conflict from which they are fleeing and the actions of the host country and international organizations. Such perceptions may change over time, depending on the international actions involved and talks between the host and sending countries. For example, Myanmar and Bangladesh are currently holding talks on economic cooperation. The media have noted the omission of Rohingya repatriation from the agenda, which the media then present as a signal that the refugees will remain in Bangladesh indefinitely. Thus, the survey of newspapers provides a sense of how long refugees are expected to stay in any given year.

It is difficult to assess whether the host governments of refugees share the media's assessment, however. Given that the newspapers I access are national dailies, I am assuming that such assessments are widely understood and accepted. Also, given that refugees know what kind of conflict they are fleeing and whether repatriation/resettlement is an option, I can fairly assume that their perception and the media's portrayal will be congruent.

Host aggression/host hostility: I checked to see whether the host government has sponsored attacks on refugees in refugee camps in each given year. The host government can be represented by border patrol, local law enforcement (e.g., police), or government paramilitary or military units. In the case of the Rohingya, there are often allegations of police brutality reported in the media; these count as acts of host aggression. However, in order to rule out "accidents," I checked to see whether at least three such incidents of host-sponsored attacks have taken place. Three is an arbitrary number, but is more informative than counting one incident of host-sponsored violence as host aggression. If there are at least three media repots, host aggression is coded as 1. Given that only high-profile refugee stories make it into the national news, three incidents suffice to prove host aggression.

Alliance: In order to understand the host's incentives to protect refugees, its relationship with the refugee-sending country becomes important. India's sour relationship with Pakistan, for example, partly contributed to the Indian government's sympathy for Bangalis fleeing military oppression in Pakistan. While the relationship between India and Pakistan has been marred by rivalry, since 1947 there have been years when the relationship was more positive and both governments tried to bridge their differences. The Samjhauta Express railway service between Lahore, Pakistan, and Amritsar India, that commenced in 1976 is one such example of cooperation.

The relevant pairs of countries in this study are: Bangladesh-Myanmar, Bangladesh-India, Bangladesh-Pakistan, India-Sri Lanka, India-China, and Pakistan-Afghanistan. There are no formal alliances between any of the pairs (such as defense pacts or treaties), but they all claim to have good relations, with the exception of Bangladesh and Pakistan in the 1970s. In order to introduce variation, I code the "status quo" times as 0, times when there are border disputes as 1 (bad relations), and times of state-level visits as 2 (good relations) in Chapter 4. In Capter 3, I code alliance as 1 when relations are good or neutral, and as 0 otherwise.

Location: The location of camps becomes especially important when separatist interests are at hand. For example, if the camps are near the border, arguably, rebels from the sending country can easily enter the refugee camps and militarize them. I code the variable as 1 when the refugee camps are within fifty miles of the border with the sending country, and 0 otherwise. There is some variation over time, even among the same refugee groups. For example, after the India government realized that Sri Lankan refugee camps had been militarized, it relocated the camps away from the border and away from one another. Thus, while most camps have semipermanent structures (such as the Bihari camp in Dhaka), this may not always be the case.

Rate of refugee inflow: This is a tally of the number of new refugees each year from one country to another, depending on the refugee group. This variable serves to check whether fresh arrivals of people keep their cause alive for a longer period of time, getting rid of the fatigue that may plague refugees after several years of encampment. The data on this is not sourced from newspapers but from UNHCR's statistics division. I also have a dichotomous version of this variable in which I code years where the number of new refugees exceeded 1,000 persons as 1 and 0 otherwise.

Shared ethnicity: I created this variable by checking to see whether a given refugee group's ethnicity matches the ethnicity of any of the ethnic groups (minority or majority) in the host country. In order to code this variable, I used the *CIA World Factbook* to identify the ethnic groups that exist in the three countries and then compared the list with the refugee groups' ethnicities, which I obtained from the UNHCR database.

Poor living conditions: I coded refugee groups as living under poor conditions based on newspaper reports regarding population density and sanitation. While in more recent years some of the reports included actual numbers (such as how many toilets per 1,000 people or the number of toilets available for a given refugee group), most of the news reports used terms such as "overcrowded," "densely populated," "lacks sanitation facilities," and so on.

Natural disasters: For the three countries under consideration, I checked to see whether in any given year cyclones/hurricanes, floods, or earthquakes took place. I used the BBC News website to gather this information. All events coded had a death toll of at least 100 people.

Aid: For the purposes of Chapter 3 and Chapter 4, what is important is not how much aid the host government receives in total, but how much aid is provided for the refugees and for refugee protection. I therefore used the UNHCR's Global Reports for all the relevant years to access the UNHCR budget for each country in any given year. There were many years during which some countries received no aid. The reports do not indicate which body was in charge of distributing aid.

International organizations: All three countries publish a list of international organizations present in the country every year. This list is provided by the government and published in the national telephone directory. I used the directory to check the years during which UNHCR operated in any given country. The years identify the refugee groups for which they are responsible. For example, in all the years that UNHCR was active in Pakistan, it was working with Afghan refugees. In the years when a country hosted multiple refugee groups (India with Tamils from Sri Lanka and Tibetans from China, for example), I checked UNHCR's online archives to determine which refugee group(s) had fallen under UNHCR's mandate.

Although the data suffers from some problems, as noted, it provides the ability to analyze two forms of refugee behavior that are often labeled "violent," namely protests and militarization. Accordingly, this dataset is used in Chapter 3 to analyze protest behavior and in Chapter 4 to analyze the militarization of refugee camps.

Notes

1 BBC Monitoring Online database. Available at: www.bbcmonitoringonline.com/mmu/.
2 From 2000 to 2006.
3 From 1971 to 2000.

Chronology

Year	Domestic Politics			International Events
	India	Pakistan	Bangladesh	
1947				India gains independence as British rule ends. Muslim state of East and West Pakistan created out of partition of India. Hundreds of thousands die in widespread communal violence and millions are made homeless. Eight million leave Pakistan for India. Seven million leave India for Pakistan.
1948	Mahatma Gandhi assassinated.	Muhammad Ali Jinnah, founding leader of Pakistan, dies.		First war between India and Pakistan over disputed territory of Kashmir.
1949		Awami League (AL) is established to campaign for East Pakistan's autonomy from West Pakistan.		
1951		Jinnah's successor Liaquat Ali Khan is assassinated.		Tibetan leaders forced to sign the Seventeen-Point Agreement, a treaty dictated by China that professes to guarantee Tibetan autonomy and to respect Buddhism, but also allows the establishment of Chinese civil and military headquarters at Lhasa. Armed resistance builds up.
1953				Korean War
1954				The Dalai Lama visits Beijing for talks with Mao, but China fails to honor the Seventeen-Point Agreement.

(*continued on the next page*)

Chronology (continued)

Year	Domestic Politics			International Events
	India	Pakistan	Bangladesh	
1955				The US invasion of Vietnam begins. Burma, India, Indonesia, Yugoslavia, and Egypt cofound the Non-Aligned Movement.
1956		Constitution proclaims Pakistan an Islamic republic.		
1958		Martial law declared; General Ayub Khan takes over.		
1959				Full-scale uprising breaks out in Lhasa. Thousands reportedly die during the suppression of the revolt. The Dalai Lama and most of his ministers flee to northern India. Eighty thousand Tibetans flee to India as refugees.
1962				China and India go to war; India subsequently defeated. Cuban Missile Crisis.
1964	Prime Minister Jawaharlal Nehru dies.			
1965	Naxal movement begins.			Chinese government establishes Tibetan Autonomous Region.
1965				Second India-Pakistan War.

Chronology (continued)

Year	Domestic Politics			International Events
	India	Pakistan	Bangladesh	
1966	Indira Gandhi becomes prime minister.			Cultural Revolution reaches Tibet, resulting in the destruction of a large number of monasteries and cultural artifacts.
1969		General Ayub Khan resigns; General Yahya Khan takes over.		
1970		The AL, under Sheikh Mujibur Rahman, wins general election. West Pakistan's government refuses to transfer power. Cyclone hits East Pakistan—up to 500,000 people are killed.		
1971	India signs twenty-year treaty of friendship with the Soviet Union.		Sheikh Mujib arrested and taken to West Pakistan. In exile, the AL declares the independence of Bangladesh on March 26.	Ten million Bangladeshi refugees flee to India. India assists the Bangladesh Mukti Bahini in defeating Pakistan. Third India-Pakistan War. Fifty thousand Biharis left behind in Bangladesh.
1972			Sheikh Mujib returns and becomes prime minister. Period of nationalization.	Military junta takes control of Burma.
1973		Zulfikar Ali Bhutto becomes prime minister.		The United States ends military involvement in Vietnam, Cambodia, and Laos.

(continued on the next page)

Chronology (continued)

| Year | Domestic Politics | | | International Events |
	India	Pakistan	Bangladesh	
1974	India conducts first underground nuclear test.		Severe floods kill 28,000 people.	
1975	Prime Minister Indira Gandhi declares state of emergency; crackdown on Naxalites.		Sheikh Mujib becomes president; is assassinated along with his family in a military coup in August: Martial law is imposed. The military bans trade unions.	Vietnam War ends. In Burma, the National Democratic Front is formed by regionally based minority groups.
1976			General Ziaur Rahman assumes presidency. Islam adopted in the constitution.	
1977		Riots erupt over allegations of vote-rigging by Bhutto's Pakistan People's Party (PPP). General Zia ul-Haq launches military coup.		
1978		General Zia ul-Haq becomes president, launches Islamization.		Two hundred thousand Rohingyas flee Burma and find refuge in Bangladesh.
1979		Zulfiqar Ali Bhutto hanged.	Martial law is lifted following elections, which Zia's Bangladesh National Party (BNP) wins.	
1980				US pledges military assistance to Pakistan following Soviet intervention in Afghanistan. One and a half million Afghan refugees flee to Pakistan.

Chronology (continued)

Year	Domestic Politics			International Events
	India	Pakistan	Bangladesh	
1981			Ziaur Rahman assassinated during abortive military coup.	
1982			BNP wins election; Zia is succeeded by Abdus Sattar.	Burmese law stipulates that people of non-indigenous background are "associate citizens." Rohingyas declared "non-national" or "foreign residents." Ethnic groups flee to India, Bangladesh, and Thailand.
1983			General Hussain Muhammad Ershad becomes president following a military coup.	First Eelam War in Sri Lanka. More than 100,000 Tamils flee ethnic cleansing. Indian intelligence begins providing covert military assistance to the LTTE.
1984	Indira Gandhi assassinated by Sikh bodyguards. Son Rajiv Gandhi takes over. Bhopal accident.			
1985		Martial law and political parties ban lifted.		
1986		Zulfikar Ali Bhutto's daughter Benazir Bhutto returns from exile to lead PPP in campaign for fresh elections.	Parliamentary and presidential elections. Ershad elected to a five-year term, lifts martial law and reinstates the constitution.	

(continued on the next page)

Chronology (continued)

Year	Domestic Politics			International Events
	India	Pakistan	Bangladesh	
1987			State of emergency declared after opposition demonstrations and strikes.	Dalai Lama calls for the establishment of Tibet as a zone of peace and continues to seek dialogue with China, with the aim of achieving genuine self-rule for Tibet within China. India deploys troops for peacekeeping operation in Sri Lanka's ethnic conflict.
1988		General Zia, the US ambassador, and top Pakistan army officials die in mysterious air crash in August. Benazir Bhutto's PPP wins November general election.	Islam becomes state religion. Floods cover up to three-quarters of the country. Tens of millions made homeless.	China imposes martial law after riots break out. In Burma, thousands of people are killed in anti-government riots. State Law and Order Restoration Council (SLORC) formed. People start fleeing to neighboring countries. Bhutan brands many ethnic Nepalis as illegal immigrants, stresses Tibetan-based Bhutanese culture. Eighty thousand flee to India and are then diverted to Nepal.
1989				Dalai Lama awarded the Nobel Peace Prize. One hundred and twenty-two thousand Tamils flee Sri Lanka and find refuge in India.
1990		Benazir Bhutto dismissed as prime minister on charges of incompetence and corruption.		

Chronology (continued)

Year	Domestic Politics			International Events
	India	Pakistan	Bangladesh	
1991	Rajiv Gandhi assassinated by suicide bomber sympathetic to Sri Lanka's Tamil Tigers. Prime Minister P. V. Narasimha Rao begins economic reform program.	Following elections, Nawaz Sharif becomes prime minister. Prime Minister Nawaz Sharif begins economic liberalization. Islamic Sharia law formally incorporated into legal code.	Ershad steps down following mass protests. Ershad convicted and jailed for corruption and illegal possession of weapons. Bi-elections instate parliamentary democracy. Begum Khaleda Zia, widow of President Zia Rahman, becomes prime minister. Cyclonic tidal wave kills up to 138,000 people.	Indian troops withdraw from Sri Lanka. Second Eelam War.
1992	Hindu extremists demolish mosque in Ayodhya, triggering widespread Hindu-Muslim violence.	Government launches campaign to stamp out violence by Urdu-speaking supporters of the Muhajir Quami Movement.		
1993		Benazir Bhutto becomes prime minister following general election.		Talks between China and the Dalai Lama break down.
1995				Third Eelam War. Fifty-five thousand Sri Lankan Tamils find refuge in India.

(continued on the next page)

Chronology (continued)

Year	Domestic Politics			International Events
	India	Pakistan	Bangladesh	
1996	Congress suffers worst ever electoral defeat; Hindu-nationalist BJP emerges as largest single party.	President Farooq Leghari dismisses Bhutto's government amid corruption allegations.	The AL wins elections; Sheikh Hasina Wajed, daughter of Sheikh Mujibur Rahman, becomes prime minister.	
1997		Nawaz Sharif returns as prime minister after his Pakistan Muslim League (PML) party wins elections.		Sixty-four thousand indigenous people from Bangladesh seek refuge in India following conflict with local Bangalis.
1998	India carries out nuclear tests, leading to widespread international condemnation.	Pakistan conducts its own nuclear tests after India explodes several nuclear devices.	Two-thirds of the country devastated by the worst floods ever. Fifteen former army officers sentenced to death for involvement in assassination of President Mujib in 1975.	The United States imposes sanctions on India and Pakistan in response to nuclear tests.
1999	Prime Minister Atal Bihari Vajpayee makes historic bus trip to Pakistan to meet Premier Nawaz Sharif and to sign bilateral Lahore peace declaration.	Benazir Bhutto and her husband convicted of corruption in April and given jail sentences. Ms. Bhutto goes into exile. General Pervez Musharraf seizes power in October coup.		Fourth India Pakistan War begins in Kargil as Pakistan-backed forces clash with the Indian military in Indian-held Kashmir. More than 1,000 killed on both sides.

Chronology (continued)

Year	Domestic Politics			International Events
	Pakistan	India	Bangladesh	
2000		US President Bill Clinton visits India to improve ties.		Sheikh Hasina criticizes military regimes in a UN speech, prompting Pakistani leader General Musharraf to cancel talks with her. Relations between Bangladesh and Pakistan strained further by row over leaked Pakistani report on 1971 War of Independence.
2001	Musharraf names himself president while remaining head of the army.		Seven killed in April bomb blast at a Bangali New Year concert in Dhaka. Hasina steps down in July and hands power to caretaker authority, becoming the first prime minister in the country's history to complete a five-year term. In October Hasina loses at polls to Khaleda Zia's BNP and its three coalition partners.	Sixteen Indian and three Bangladeshi soldiers are killed in border clashes. July. India Prime Minister Vajpayee meets Pakistani President Pervez Musharraf; talks end without a breakthrough owing to differences over Kashmir. September 11 terrorist attacks on United States kill 3,000; United States declares "war on terror" and invades Afghanistan, with support of India and Pakistan. United States lifts sanctions on both countries in return. More than two million Afghan refugees flee to Pakistan. The Dalai Lama and Beijing resume contact.
2002		India test-fires a nuclear-capable ballistic missile. Fifty-nine Hindu pilgrims killed in a train fire in Gujarat. More than 1,000 Muslims die in ensuing violence.		

(continued on the next page)

Chronology (continued)

Year	Domestic Politics			International Events
	India	Pakistan	Bangladesh	
2002		In April election, Musharraf wins another five years "unconstitutionally" and grants himself new powers, including the right to dismiss an elected parliament. Pakistan test-fires three medium-range surface-to-surface missiles capable of carrying nuclear warheads.	March: Government introduces law making acid attacks punishable by death.	Aggressive language between Indian and Pakistani leaders creates fears of war. Pakistani President Musharraf visits Bangladesh in July and expresses regret over Pakistan's role during 1971 War of Independence.
2003				US invades Iraq. Pakistan declares a Kashmir ceasefire; India follows suit.
2004	Surprise victory for Congress Party in general elections makes Manmohan Singh prime minister. India, along with Brazil, Germany and Japan, launches an application for a permanent seat on the UN Security Council.		Parliament amends constitution to reserve forty-five seats for female MPs. Grenade attack on opposition AL rally in Dhaka kills twenty-two. AL leader Sheikh Hasina survives the attack.	Pakistan mounts first military offensive against suspected al-Qaeda militants and their supporters in tribal areas near Afghan border in June. US begins using drone strikes to target al-Qaeda leaders in the area. A tsunami causes devastation in southeast Asia.

Chronology (continued)

Year	Domestic Politics			International Events
	India	Pakistan	Bangladesh	
2005		Pakistan tests its first nuclear-capable cruise missile.	In January prominent AL politician Shah A. M. S. Kibria is killed in a grenade attack at a political rally. AL calls a general strike in protest. On August 17 around 350 small bombs go off in towns and cities nationwide. Two people are killed and more than 100 are injured. A banned Islamic group claims responsibility.	Bus service between Srinagar in Indian-administered Kashmir and Muzaffarabad in Pakistani-administered Kashmir resumes for the first time in sixty years.
2006	On July 11 more than 180 people killed in bomb attacks on rush-hour trains in Mumbai. Investigators blame Islamic militants based in Pakistan.		Violent protests over government's choice of a caretaker administration to take over when Premier Zia completes her term at the end of October. President Ahmed assumes caretaker role for period leading up to January 2007 elections.	The United States and India sign a nuclear agreement during a visit by US President George W. Bush. The United States gives India access to civilian nuclear technology while India agrees to greater scrutiny of its nuclear program. Hu Jintao makes the first visit to India by a Chinese president in a decade. Bush approves a controversial law allowing India to buy US nuclear reactors and fuel for the first time in thirty years.

(*continued on the next page*)

Chronology (continued)

Year	India	Pakistan	Bangladesh	International Events
	India	*Pakistan*	*Bangladesh*	*International Events*
2007	Maoist rebels in Chhattisgarh state kill more than fifty policemen in a dawn raid in March. Government announces its biggest increase in gross domestic product for twenty years—9.4 percent.	Benazir Bhutto returns from exile. Dozens of people die in a suicide bomb targeting her homecoming parade in Karachi. Army launches offensive against militants in North Waziristan; nearly 200 die. Musharraf wins presidential election but is challenged by Supreme Court; he declares emergency rule, dismisses Chief Justice Chaudhry, and appoints new Supreme Court, which confirms his re-election. In December, Benazir Bhutto assassinated at election campaign rally in Rawalpindi.	In January, a state of emergency is declared amid violence in the election run-up. President Fakhruddin Ahmed postpones elections and heads caretaker administration. Six Islamist militants convicted of the 2005 bomb attacks, including leaders of Jagrata Muslim Janata Bangladesh and Jamaat-ul-Mujahideen, hanged. In April Sheikh Hasina is charged with murder. Begum Khaleda Zia held under virtual house arrest. Several other politicians are held in an anti-corruption drive. Government imposes a curfew on Dhaka and five other cities amid violent August clashes between police and students demanding an end to emergency rule.	On February 18 sixty-eight passengers, mostly Pakistanis, are killed by bomb blasts on a train from New Delhi to Lahore. India and Pakistan sign an agreement aimed at reducing the risk of accidental nuclear war.

Chronology (continued)

Year	Domestic Politics			International Events
	India	Pakistan	Bangladesh	
2008	Explosions kill forty-nine in Ahmedabad; little-known group Indian Mujahideen claims responsibility. India successfully launches its first mission to the moon. Nearly 200 killed and hundreds injured in coordinated attacks on Mumbai.	February elections result in a coalition government between PPP and PML-N, with PPP nominee as prime minister. President Musharraf resigns after the two main governing parties agree to launch impeachment proceedings against him. Nawaz Sharif pulls his PML-N party out of the coalition for not reinstating judges sacked by Musharraf. Asif Ali Zardari, widower of Benazir Bhutto, becomes president. Pakistan borrows billions of dollars from the International Monetary Fund to overcome its debt crisis.	Cyclone Sidr hits. AL captures more than 250 of 300 seats in parliament. Sheikh Hasina is sworn in as prime minister in January.	Bush ends a three-decade ban on US nuclear trade with Delhi. India blames Mumbai attacks on Pakistani-based militants and demands that Pakistan take action. Islamabad denies involvement but promises to cooperate with the Indian investigation. India announces "pause" in peace process with Pakistan. Indian cricket team cancels planned tour of Pakistan.

(continued on the next page)

Chronology (continued)

Year	Domestic Politics			International Events
	India	Pakistan	Bangladesh	
2009	Governing Congress-led alliance of Prime Minister Manmohan Singh wins enhanced position in parliament, only eleven seats short of an absolute majority. Government agrees to allow a new state, Telangana, to be carved out of part of the southern state of Andhra Pradesh. Violent protests for and against break out.	Government agrees to implement Sharia law in northwestern Swat valley in effort to persuade Islamist militants there to agree to permanent ceasefire. Swat agreement breaks down after Taliban-linked militants seek to extend their control. Government launches offensive to wrest control of Swat from militants. Supreme Court acquits Nawaz Sharif of hijacking charges dating from 1999 army coup, removing ban on his running for public office. Suicide bombing in northwestern city of Peshawar kills 120 people.	Seventy-four people, mainly army officers, are killed in a February mutiny in Dhaka by border guards unhappy with pay and conditions. Police arrest 700 guards. A further 1,000 are detained in May.	India and Russia sign uranium deals worth US $700m. Pakistani, Indian premiers pledge to work together to fight terror irrespective of progress on improving broader ties. Baitullah Mehsud, leader of Pakistan's Taliban, killed in US drone attack in South Waziristan; is succeeded by Hakimullah Mehsud.
2010		Worst floods in eighty years kill at least 1,600 people and affect more than twenty million. Government response widely criticized.		

Chronology (continued)

Year	Domestic Politics			International Events
	India	*Pakistan*	*Bangladesh*	
2011	India overtakes China to become the world's largest importer of arms.			The prime ministers of India and Pakistan meet to watch a cricket match and repair relations. Al-Qaeda founder Osama bin Laden killed by American special forces in Abbottabad. Pakistan shuts down NATO supply routes after a NATO attack on military outposts kills twenty-five Pakistani soldiers.
2012		Supreme Court disqualifies Prime Minister Yousuf Raza Gilani from holding office after he declines to appeal against a token sentence in President Zardari corruption row. Parliament approves Minister of Water and Power Raja Pervez Ashraf as his successor.	Buddhist temples burnt down in Ramu, Cox's Bazar.	Fresh refugees flee attacks in Myanmar. Bangladesh closes borders. Pakistan boycotts the Bonn Conference on Afghanistan in protest at the NATO attack on a border checkpoint. Pakistani government comes under pressure over a leaked memo alleging that senior officials sought US aid against a military coup after the killing of Osama bin Laden. US troops leave the Shamsi air base in Balochistan; Pakistan blocks US convoys from entering Afghanistan. Manmohan Singh pays first official visit to Burma by an Indian prime minister since 1987 and signs agreements aimed at providing border area development and an Indian credit line. Pakistan agrees to reopen NATO supply routes to Afghanistan after the United States apologizes.

Bibliography

Achvarina, V., and S. F. Reich. 2006. "No Place to Hide: Refugees, Displaced Persons, and the Recruitment of Child Soldiers." *International Security* 33(1): 127–64.

Adelman, H. 1998. "Why Refugee Warriors Are Threats." *Journal of Conflict Studies* 18 (1). Available at: http://journals.hil.unb.ca/index.php/JCS/article/view/11672/12402.

Alavi, H. 1989. "Nationhood and the Nationalities in Pakistan." *Economic and Political Weekly* 24(27): 1527–34.

Amnesty International. 2000. "Bangladesh: Human Rights in the Chittagong Hill Tracts." Section 5.2. Amnesty International website, February 1. Available at: http://web.archive.org/web/20041031203114/http://web.amnesty.org/library/Index/engASA130012000.

Anderson, B. 1983. *Imagined Communities: Reflections on the Origin and Spread of Nationalism.* New York: Verso.

Arendt, H. 1943. "We Refugees." Menorah Journal, 31(1), 69–77.

Bakewell, O. 2001. "Refugee Aid and Protection in Rural Africa: Working in Parallel or Cross-Purposes?" *New Issues in Refugee Research: Working Paper No. 35.* Geneva: UNHCR Evaluation and Policy Analysis Unit.

Bandyopadhyay, S. 1999. "Changing Borders, Shifting Loyalties: Religion, Caste and the Partition of Bengal in 1947." Wellington, New Zealand: Asian Studies Institute. Available at: www.victoria.ac.nz/slc/asi/publications/02-changing-borders.pdf.

Barber, B. 1997. "Feeding Refugees, or War? The Dilemma of Humanitarian Aid." *Foreign Affairs* 76(4): 8–14.

Baron, N., S. B. Jensen, and J. T. Jong. 2003. "Refugees and Internally Displaced People." In *Trauma Interventions in War and Peace*, eds. Bonnie L. Green, Matthew J. Friedman, Joop de Jong, Susan D. Solomon, Terence M. Keane, John A. Fairbank, Brigid Donelan, and Ellen Frey-Wouters. New York: Springer, 243–70.

Bennett, S. D., and A. C. Stam III. 1996. "The Declining Advantages of Democracy: A Combined Model of War Outcomes and Duration." *Journal of Conflict Resolution* 42(3): 344–66.

Bharadwaj, P., A. Khwaja, and A. Mian. 2008. "The Big March: Nature of the Migratory Flows after Partition of British India." *Economic and Political Weekly* 43 (35): 39–49.

Bull, H. 1984. *Intervention in International Politics.* New York: Oxford University Press.

Butalia, U. 2001. *Other Side of Silence: Voices from the Partition of India.* New Delhi: Penguin.

Cambers, R. 1982. "Rural Refugees in Africa: Past Experience, Future Pointers." *Disasters* 6(1): 21–30.

Central Intelligence Agency (CIA). The World Factbook. Available at: www.cia.gov/library/publications/the-world-factbook/.

Central Statistical Organisation. 2005. *Provisional Results of Economic Census 2005: All India Report*. New Delhi: Government of India, Ministry of Statistics and Programme Implementation, Central Statistical Organisation. Available at: http://mospi.nic.in/mospi_new/upload/economic_census_prov_results_2005.pdf.

Chakrabarty, P. K. 1999. *The Marginal Men: The Refugees and the Left Political Syndrome in West Bengal*. Calcutta: Naya Udyog and Lumiere Books.

Chatterjee, N. 2002. "Interrogating Victimhood: East Bengali Refugee Narratives of Communal Violence." London: Swadhinata Trust. Available at: www.swadhinata.org.uk/document/chatterjeeEastBengal%20Refugee.pdf.

Chatterjee, P. 1986. *Nationalist Thought and the Colonial World: A Derivative Discourse*. Minneapolis, MN: University of Minnesota Press.

Chatterji, J. 2007. "Dispersal and the Failure of Rehabilitation: Refugee Camp-Dwellers and Squatters in West Bengal." *Modern Asian Studies* 41(5): 995–1032.

Chaturvedi, S. 2002. "Process of Othering in the Case of India and Pakistan." *Tijdschrift voor Economische en Sociale Geografie* 93(2): 149–59.

Chaulia, S. S. 2003. "The Politics of Refugee Hosting in Tanzania: From Open Door to Unsustainability, Insecurity and Receding Receptivity." *Journal of Refugee Studies,* 16(2): 147–66.

Chenoy, K. M., and A. M. Chenoy. 2007. "India's Foreign Policy Shifts and the Calculus of Power." *Economic and Political Weekly* 42(35): 3547–54.

Clark, J. A., and J. S. Legge. 1997. "Economics, Racism, and Attitudes toward Immigration in the New Germany." *Political Research Quarterly* 50(4): 901–17.

Coll, S. 2005. *Ghost Wars: The Secret History of the CIA, Afghanistan, and Bin Laden, from the Soviet Invasion to September 10, 2001*. New York: Penguin.

Collier, P. 1999. "On the Economic Consequences of Civil War." *Oxford Economic Papers* 51: 168–83.

Collier, P., and A. Hoeffler. 2004. "Greed and Grievance in Civil War." *Oxford Economic Papers* 56(4): 563–95.

Crossette, B. 2002. "Sri Lanka: In the Shadow of the Indian Elephant." *World Policy Journal* 19(1): 25–35.

Daily Star. 2012a. "MKA Hints at Rohingya Link With Ramu Violence." *Daily Star*, October 1. Available at: www.thedailystar.net/newDesign/latest_news.php?nid=41299.

——2012b. "4 Bangladeshis Shot by BSF." *Daily Star*, November 5. Available at: www.thedailystar.net/newDesign/news-details.php?nid=256304.

——2012c. "BSF Picks Up Two Bangladeshi Cattle Traders." *Daily Star*, December 12. Available at: www.thedailystar.net/newDesign/news-details.php?nid=263039.

Davis, D., and W. H. Moore. 1997. "Ethnicity Matters: Transnational Ethnic Alliances and Foreign Policy Behavior." *International Studies Quarterly* 41(1): 171–84.

Destradi, S. 2012. "India and Sri Lanka's Civil War." *Asian Survey* 52(3): 595–616.

Dorman, A. M., and T. G. Otte, eds. 1995. *Military Intervention: From Gunboat Diplomacy to Humanitarian Intervention*. Aldershot: Dartmouth Press.

Dowty, A., and G. Loescher. 1996. "Refugee Flows as Grounds for International Action." *International Security* 21: 43–71.

Doyle, M. W., and N. Sambanis. 2000. "International Peace-Building: A Theoretical and Quantitative Analysis." *American Political Science Review* 94: 779–802.

Dupree, N. H. 1988. "Demographic Reporting on Afghan Refugees in Pakistan." *Modern Asian Studies* 22(4): 845–65.

Dutta, N. 2012. "The Myth of the Bangladeshi and Violence in Assam." *Kafila,* August 16. Available at: http://kafila.org/2012/08/16/the-myth-of-the-bangladeshi-and-violence-in-assam-nilim-dutta/.

Elbadawi, I., and N. Sambanis. 2002. "How Much War Will We See? Explaining the Prevalence of Civil War." *Journal of Conflict Resolution* 46(3): 307–34.

Ennals, D. 1982. "The Biharis in 1981." In *The Biharis in Bangladesh,* ed. Ben Whitaker, Iain Guest, and David Ennals. London: Minority Rights Group, 30.

Far Eastern Economic Review. 1971. "Who Is My Neighbor?" *Far Eastern Economic Review* 73(35): 80. Available at: www.nybangla.com/weekly%201971/August/4th%20Week/far_eastern_economic_review.htm.

Farzana, K. 2008. "The Neglected Stateless Bihari Community in Bangladesh: Victims of Political and Diplomatic Onslaught." *Journal of Humanities and Social Sciences* 2(1).

Fearon, J. D. 2004. "Why Do Some Civil Wars Last So Much Longer than Others?" *Journal of Peace Research* 41(3): 275–301.

Fearon, J. D., and D. D. Laitin. 2003. "Ethnicity, Insurgency, and Civil War." *American Political Science Review* 97: 75–90.

Fetzer, J. S. 2000. *Public Attitudes toward Immigration in the United States, France, and Germany.* Cambridge: Cambridge University Press.

George, R. 2011. "Life in Limbo for Chin Refugees." *New York Times,* November 30. Available at: http://india.blogs.nytimes.com/2011/11/30/life-in-limbo-for-chin-refugees/.

Gilmartin, D. 1998. "Partition, Pakistan, and South Asian History: In Search of a Narrative." *Journal of Asian Studies* 57(4): 1068–95.

Giugni, M., D. McAdam, and C. Tilly. 1999. *How Social Movements Matter.* Minneapolis, MN: University of Minnesota Press.

Goldstone, J. A., and C. Tilly. 2001. "Threat (and Opportunity): Popular Action and State Response in the Dynamics of Contentious Action." In *Silence and Voice in the Study of Contentious Politics,* eds. Ronald R. Aminzade, Jack A. Goldstone, Doug McAdam, and Elizabeth J. Perry. Cambridge: Cambridge University Press, 179–94.

Guest, I. (1982) "The Context of Bangladesh in 1977." In *The Biharis in Bangladesh,* eds. Ben Whitaker, Iain Guest, and David Ennals. London: Minority Rights Group, 25.

Guhathakurta, M. 2011. "Partnerships and Solutions for Protracted Refugee Situations." In *UNHCR Panel Report, 2011.* Dhaka: UNHCR.

Gupta, K. 1978. "Sino-Indian Agreement on Tibetan Trade and Intercourse: Its Origin and Significance." *Economic and Political Weekly* 13(16): 696–702.

——1980. "Distortions in the History of Sino-Indian Frontiers." *Economic and Political Weekly* 15(30): 1265, 1267–70.

——1982. "India-China Border." *Economic and Political Weekly* 17(32): 1291–92.

Gunaratna, R. 1993. *Indian Intervention in Sri Lanka: The Role of India's Intelligence Agencies,* Colombo: South Asian Network on Conflict Research.

Gurr, T. R. 1970. *Why Men Rebel.* Boulder, CO: Paradigm Publishers.

Guruswamy, M. 2003. "India-China Border Learning from History." *Economic and Political Weekly* 38(39): 4101–3.

Habib, H. 2011. "Bangladesh Honours Indira Gandhi with Highest Award." *Hindu,* July 25. Available at: www.thehindu.com/news/international/article2293016.ece.

Hainmueller, J., and M. J. Hiscox. 2010. "Attitudes toward Highly Skilled and Low-Skilled Immigration: Evidence from a Survey Experiment." *American Political Science Review* 104(1): 61–84.

Haq, F. 1995. "Rise of the MQM in Pakistan: Politics of Ethnic Mobilization." *Asian Survey* 35(11): 990–1004.

Hernes, G., and K. Knudsen. 1992. "Norwegians' Attitudes toward New Immigrants." *Acta Sociologica* 35: 123–39.

Hibbs, D. 1973. *Mass Political Violence: A Cross-National Causal Analysis.* Boston, MA: MIT Press.

Human Rights Commission of Pakistan. 2009. *State of Human Rights in 2009.* Lahore: Human Rights Commission of Pakistan. Available at: www.hrcp-web.org/pdf/areports/11.pdf.

Human Rights Watch. 1996. "Burma: The Rohingya Muslims: Ending a Cycle of Exodus?" Human Rights Watch web site, C809, September 1. Available at: www.unhcr.org/refworld/docid/3ae6a84a2.html.

Hussain, A. 1987. "Karachi Riots of December 1986: Crisis of State and Civil Society in Pakistan." *Economic and Political Weekly* 22(11): 450–51.

Hussain, K. T. 1971. "Sino-Indian Relations." Economic and Political Weekly 6(38): 2017–22.

International Committee for the Stranded Pakistanis (Biharis) in Bangladesh. 1997. "Briefing Paper on Biharis in Bangladesh." International Committee for the Stranded Pakistanis (Biharis) in Bangladesh, June, 4.

Jacobsen, K. 1996. "Factors Influencing the Policy Responses of Host Governments to Mass Refugee Influxes." *International Migration Review* 30(3): 655–78.

James, L. R. 2000. *Raj: The Making and Unmaking of British India.* New York: St. Martin's Griffin.

Jones, R. 2009. "Geopolitical Boundary Narratives, the Global War on Terror and Border Fencing in India." *Transactions of the Institute of British Geographers* 34(3): 290–304.

Kalyvas, S. N. 2006. *The Logic of Violence in Civil War.* Cambridge: Cambridge University Press, 371.

Kaufmann, C. 1996. "Possible and Impossible Solutions to Ethnic Civil Wars." *International Security* 20(4): 136–75.

Kaur, R. 2006. "The Last Journey: Exploring Social Class in the 1947 Partition Migration." *Economic and Political Weekly* 41(22): 2221–28.

Kessler, T., A. Mummendey, F. Funke, R. Brown, J. Binder, H. Zagefka, J. Leyens, S. Demoulin, and A. Maquil. 2010. "'We All Live in Germany But …': Ingroup Projection, Group-Based Emotions and Prejudice against Immigrants." *European Journal of Social Psychology* 40(6): 985–97.

Khalidi, O. 1998. "From Torrent to Trickle: Indian Muslim Migration to Pakistan, 1947–97." *Islamic Studies* 37(3): 339–52.

Khan, Y. 2007. *The Great Partition: The Making of India and Pakistan.* New Haven, CT: Yale University Press.

Kitschelt, H. 1986. "Political Opportunity Structures and Political Protest: Anti-Nuclear Movements in Four Democracies." *British Journal of Political Science* 16(1): 57–85.

Koo, E. 2010. "Kathmandu's Tibetan Refugees Protest against China on the 51st Anniversary of 1959 Uprising." *Demotix*, March 10. Available at: www.demotix.com/news/272437/kathmandus-tibetan-refugees-protest-against-china-51st-anniversary-1959-uprising#slide-1.

Koser, K. 2011. " Internally Displaced Persons." In *Global Migration Governance,* ed. Alexander Betts. Oxford and New York: Oxford University Press, pp. 210–23.

Krasner, S. D. 1999. *Sovereignty: Organized Hypocrisy.* Princeton, NJ: Princeton University Press.

Kronenfeld, D. A. 2008. Afghan Refugees in Pakistan: Not All Refugees, Not Always in Pakistan, Not Necessarily Afghan? *Journal of Refugee Studies*, 21(1), 43–63.

Kunz, E. F. 1981. "Exile and Resettlement: Refugee Theory." *International Migration Review* 15(1/2): 42–51.

Lake, D. A., and D. S. Rothchild, eds. 1998. *The International Spread of Ethnic Conflict: Fear, Diffusion, and Escalation.* Princeton, NJ: Princeton University Press.

Leenders, R. (2009). Refugee Warriors or War Refugees? Iraqi Refugees' Predicament in Syria, Jordan and Lebanon. *Mediterranean Politics,* 14(3), 343–63

Levie, H. S. 1974. "The Indo-Pakistani Agreement of August 28, 1973." *American Journal of International Law* 68(1): 95–97.

Lichbach, M. I. 1987. "Deterrence or Escalation? The Puzzle of Aggregate Studies of Repression and Dissent." *Journal of Conflict Resolution* 31(2), 266–97.

Lipsky, M. 1968. "Protest as a Political Resource." *American Political Science Review* 62(4): 1144–58.

Lischer, S. K. 2003. "Collateral Damage: Humanitarian Assistance as a Cause of Conflict." *International Security* 28(1): 79–109.

——2005. *Dangerous Sanctuaries: Refugee Camps, Civil War, and the Dilemmas of Humanitarian Aid.* Ithaca, NY: Cornell University Press.

Loescher, G. 1989. *Beyond Charity: International Cooperation and the Global Refugee Crisis.* New York: Oxford University Press.

——2001. "The UNHCR and World Politics: State Interests vs. Institutional Autonomy." *International Migration Review* 35(1): 33–56.

Loescher, G., and J. Milner. 2005. "Security Implications of Protracted Refugee Situations." *Adelphi Papers* 45(375): 23–34.

Loescher, G., and L. Monahan. 1989. *Refugees and International Relations.* New York: Clarendon Press.

Loescher, G., A. Betts, and J. Milner. 2008. *UNHCR: The Politics and Practice of Refugee Protection Into the 21st Century.* New York: Routledge.

Mamdani, M. 2002. *When Victims Become Killers.* Princeton, NJ: Princeton University Press.

Manto, S. H. 1987. *Kingdom's End and Other Stories.* New Delhi: Penguin.

Marsden, M. 2005. "Mullahs, Migrants and Murids: New Developments in the Study of Pakistan: A Review Article." *Modern Asian Studies* 39(4): 981–1005.

Marwah, O. 1979. "India's Military Intervention in East Pakistan, 1971–72. *Modern Asian Studies* 13: 549–80.

Matinuddin, K. (2000). *The Taliban Phenomenon: Afghanistan 1994–1997.* Karachi: Oxford University Press.

Maxwell, N. 1999. "Sino-Indian Border Dispute Reconsidered." *Economic and Political Weekly* 34(15): 905–18.

Mayda, A. M. 2006. "Who Is Against Immigration? A Cross-Country Investigation of Individual Attitudes toward Immigrants." *Review of Economics and Statistics* 88: 510–30.

McAdam, D., S. Tarrow, and C. Tilly. 2001. *Dynamics of Contention.* Cambridge: Cambridge University Press.

——2008. "Methods for Measuring Mechanisms of Contention." *Qualitative Sociology* 31(4): 307–31.

Mearsheimer, J. 2003. *The Tragedy of Great Power Politics.* New York: W. W. Norton.

Meyer, D. S. 2007. *The Politics of Protests: Social Movements in America.* Oxford: Oxford University Press.

Meyer, D. S., and S. D. Tarrow. 1999. *The Social Movement Society: Contentious Politics for a New Century.* Lanham, MD: Rowman & Littlefield.

Ministry of Relief and Rehabilitation. 1997. *Latest Situation Report on the Stranded Non-Bangalis in Bangladesh.* Dhaka: Government of Bangladesh, 2.

Minorities at Risk Project. 1997. "Chronology for Chittagong Hill Tribes in Bangladesh." Minorities at Risk Project, March 9. Available at: www.unhcr.org/refworld/country, CHRON,BGD,469f38681e,0.html.

Morgenthau, H. J. 1967. "To Intervene or Not to Intervene." *Foreign Affairs* 45(3): 425.

Mukherji, P. N. 1974. "The Great Migration of 1971: I: Exodus." *Economic and Political Weekly* 9(9): 365–69.

Mukhopadhyay, K. P. 2007. *Partition, Bengal and After: The Great Tragedy of India.* New Delhi: Reference Press.

Murshid, N. 2011. "India's Role in Bangladesh's War of Independence: Humanitarianism or Self-Interest?" *Economic and Political Weekly* 46(52): 53–60.

——2012. "Refugee Camp Militarization in Bangladesh and Thailand." *Economic and Political Weekly* 47(47–48): 103–8.

Murshid, T. M. 1995. *The Sacred and the Secular: Bengal Muslim Discourses, 1871–1977.* Kolkata: Oxford University Press.

——2007. "The Forgotten Biharis: Policy Options for Their Repatriation and Rehabilitation." In *Political Culture in Bangladesh: Perspectives and Analyses,* ed. S. Andaleeb. Dhaka: University Press Ltd.

Namgyal Dolkar v. Ministry of External Affairs. 2009. 12179/2009 High Court of Delhi, India. Available at: http://indiankanoon.org/doc/994217/.

North, D. C., and B. R. Weingast. 1989. "Constitutions and Commitment: The Evolution of Institutions Governing Public Choice in Seventeenth-Century England." *Journal of Economic History* 49(04): 803–32.

O'Rourke, K. H., and R. Sinnott. 2006. "The Determinants of Individual Attitudes towards Immigration." *European Journal of Political Economy* 22(4): 838–61.

Pandey, G. 2001. *Remembering Partition: Violence, Nationalism and History in India.* Cambridge: Cambridge University Press.

Pant, H. V. 2007. "India and Bangladesh: Will the Twain Ever Meet?" *Asian Survey,* 47(2): 231–49.

Poe, S. C., and C. N. Tate. 1994. "Repression of Human Rights to Personal Integrity in the 1980s: A Global Analysis." *American Political Science Review* 88(4): 853–72.

Poppelwell, T. 2007. "Afghanistan." *Forced Migration Online.* Available at: www.forcedmigration.org/research-resources/expert-guides/afghanistan/alldocuments#section-28.

Posen, B. R. 1996. "Military Responses to Refugee Disasters." *International Security.* 21(1): 72–111.

Puri, B. 2007. "Plight of Urdu-Speaking Muslims." *Economic and Political Weekly* 42 (12): 999–1000.

Quaderi, F. Q. 1971. *Bangladesh Genocide and World Press.* Dhaka: Begum Dilafroz Quaderi.

Rahman, M., and W. V. Schendel. 2003. "'I Am Not a Refugee': Rethinking Partition Migration." *Modern Asian Studies* 37(3): 551–84.

Rasler, K. 1996. "Concessions, Repression, and Political Protest in the Iranian Revolution." *American Sociological Review* 50: 132–52.

Ray, A. K. 2001. "From Autonomy to Self-Determination: The Politics of East Pakistan and Kashmir." *Economic and Political Weekly* 36(49): 4538–43.

Raychaudhury, A. B. 2004. "Nostalgia of 'Desh,' Memories of Partition." *Economic and Political Weekly* 39(52): 5653–60.

Refugees International. 2009. *Annual Report*. Available at: www.refintl.org/who-we-are/annual-reports/2009-annual-report.

Rosenau, J. N. 1967. *Domestic Sources of Foreign Policy*. New York: Free Press.

Ross, M. R. 2004. "What Do We Know about Natural Resources and Civil War?" *Journal of Peace Research* 41: 337–56.

Saideman, S. M. 2001. *The Ties that Divide: Ethnic Politics, Foreign Policy, and International Conflict*. New York: Columbia University Press.

Salehyan, I. 2008. "The Externalities of Civil Strife: Refugees as a Source of International Conflict." *American Journal of Political Science* 52: 787–801.

Salehyan, I., and K. S. Gleditsch. 2006. "Refugees and the Spread of Civil War." *International Organization* 60(2): 335–66.

Scott, J. C. 1985. *Weapons of the Weak: Everyday Forms of Peasant Resistance*. New Haven, CT: Yale University Press.

Schweitzer, R., S. A. Perkoulidis, S. L. Krome, and C. N. Ludlow. 2005. "Attitudes towards Refugees: The Dark Side of Prejudice in Australia." *Australian Journal of Psychology* 57(3): 170–79.

Sengupta, N. 2007. *Bengal Divided: The Unmaking of a Nation 1905–1971*. New Delhi: Viking Penguin.

Shamshad, R. 2008. "Politics and Origin of the India-Bangladesh Border Fence." In *Proceedings of the 17th Biennial Conference of the Asian Studies Association of Australia, Melbourne*, July 1–3, Melbourne, Australia.

Sharma, B. 2012. "Eid Among Myanmar's Rohingyas in Delhi." *Wall Street Journal*, August 21. Available at: http://blogs.wsj.com/indiarealtime/2012/08/21/celebrating-eid-among-myanmars-rohingyas-in-delhi/.

Singh, S. K. 1999. *Bangladesh Documents*. Dhaka: University Press Ltd.

Sisson, R., and L. E. Rose. 1990. *War and Secession: Pakistan, India, and the Creation of Bangladesh*. Berkeley, CA: University of California Press.

Skocpol, T. 1979. *States and Social Revolutions* (Vol. 29). Cambridge: Cambridge University Press.

Stedman, J. S., and F. Tanner. 2003. *Refugee Manipulation: War, Politics, and the Abuse of Human Suffering*. Washington, DC: Brookings Institute Press.

Stern, R. 2001. *Democracy and Dictatorship in South Asia: Dominant Classes and Political Outcomes in India, Pakistan, and Bangladesh*. New Delhi: India Research Press.

Stiglitz, J. 2001. *Globalization and Its Discontents*. New York: W. W. Norton.

Stone, R. W. 2004. "The Political Economy of IMF Lending in Africa." *American Political Science Review* 98(04): 577–91.

Suryanarayan, V. 2009. "Focus on the Sri Lankan Tamil Refugees." *Sri Lanka Guardian*, November 13. Available at: www.srilankaguardian.org/2009/11/focus-on-sri-lankan-tamil-refugees.html.

Tagore, R. 1917. "Nationalism in India." In *Words of Freedom: Ideas of a Nation*. New Delhi: Penguin.

Tajuddin, M. 1997. "The Stateless People in Bangladesh." In *State Development and Political Culture: Bangladesh and India*, ed. B. De and R. Samaddar. New Delhi: Har-Anand Publications, 203–22.

Talbot, I. 2011. "Punjabi Refugees' Rehabilitation and the Indian State: Discourses, Denials and Dissonances." *Modern Asian Studies* 45(1): 109–30.

Tarrow, S. 1994. *Power in Movement: Social Movements, Collective Action, and Politics*. Cambridge: Cambridge University Press.

———2011. *Power in Movement: Social Movements and Contentious Politics.* Cambridge: Cambridge University Press.

Teitelbaum, M. S. 1984. "Immigration, Refugees, and Foreign Policy." *International Organizations* 38(3): 429–50.

Terry, F. 2002. *Condemned to Repeat? The Paradox of Humanitarian Action.* Ithaca, NY: Cornell University Press.

Tilly, C. 2005. *Social Movements, 1768–2004.* Boulder, CO: Paradigm Publishers.

Times of India. 2011. "Bhutan Dashes Refugees' Home-Coming Dreams." *Times of India*, April 16. Available at: http://articles.timesofindia.indiatimes.com/2011–04–16/south-asia/29424900_1_bhutanese-refugees-bhutan-s-prime-minister-nepal-and-bhutan.

———2012. "India Donates $200,000 for Riot-Hit in Myanmar's Rakhine State." *Times of India*, September 3. Available at: http://articles.timesofindia.indiatimes.com/2012-09–03/india/33562245_1_sittwe-rohingya-muslims-naypyidaw.

Timm, R. W. 1991. *The Adivasis of Bangladesh.* London: Minority Rights Group, 10.

Toor, S. 2011. *The State of Islam: Culture and Cold War Politics in Pakistan.* New York: Pluto Press.

United Nations High Commissioner for Refugees (UNCHR). 2002. *UNCHR Statistical Yearbook*, s.v. "India." New York: United Nations. Available at: www.unhcr.org/414ad5880.html.

———2003. *UNCHR Statistical Yearbook*, s.v. "Pakistan." New York: United Nations. Available at: www.unhcr.org/41d2c192c.html.

———2005. *UNCHR Statistical Yearbook*, s.v. "India." New York: United Nations.

———2010. "Text of the 1951 Convention Relating to the Status of Refugees" and "Text of the 1967 Protocol Relating to the Status of Refugees." New York: United Nations. Available at: www.unhcr.org/3b66c2aa10.html.

———2011. *UNCHR Global Appeal 2011 Update*, s.v. "India." New York: United Nations. Available at: http://www.unhcr.org/4cd96e919.html.

———2012a. *India Factsheet 2012.* New York: United Nations. Available at: http://reliefweb.int/report/india/unhcr-india-fact-sheet-february-2012.

———2012b. "2012 UNHCR Country Operations Profile – Bangladesh." UNHCR.org, available at: www.unhcr.org/cgi-bin/texis/vtx/page?page=49e487546& submit=GO.

———2012c. "2012 UNHCR Country Operations Profile – Pakistan." UNHCR.org, available at: www.unhcr.org/cgi-bin/texis/vtx/page?page=49e487016& submit=GO.

———2012d. *UNCHR Global Appeal 2012 Update*, s.v. "Pakistan." New York: United Nations. Available at: www.unhcr.org/4ec231040.html.

———2013. "2013 UNHCR Regional Operations Profile—South-East Asia: Bangladesh." New York: United Nations. Available at: www.unhcr.org/pages/49e487546.html.

United Kingdom Home Office. 2011. "Country of Origin Information Report—Bangladesh." Available at: www.unhcr.org/refworld/docid/4f0ac1831.html.

United States Committee for Refugees and Immigrants (USCRI). 2009a. "Worst Places for Refugees." In *World Refugee Survey 2009.* Arlington, VA: United States Committee for Refugees and Immigrants.

———2009b. "World Refugee Survey 2009: India." Available at: www.refugees.org/resources/refugee-warehousing/archived-world-refugee-surveys/2009-wrs-country-updates/india.html.

Van Schendel, W. 2002. "Stateless in South Asia: The Making of the India-Bangladesh Enclaves." *Journal of Asian Studies* 61(01): 115–47.

Verghese, B. G. 2012. "The War We Lost." *Tehelka* 41(9). Available at: http://tehelka.com/the-war-we-lost/.

Weiner, M. 1993. "Rejected Peoples and Unwanted Migrants in South Asia." *Economic and Political Weekly* 28(34): 1737–46.

West, R. 1997. *ICSPB Report on Biharis in Bangladesh*. June, 4.

Whitaker, B. 1982. "The Origins of the Problem." In *The Biharis in Bangladesh*, ed. Ben Whitaker, Iain Guest, and David Ennals. London: Minority Rights Group, 16–17.

Woodwell, D. 2004. "Unwelcome Neighbors: Shared Ethnicity and International Conflict During the Cold War." *International Studies Quarterly* 48(1): 197–223.

Zieck, M. 2008."The Legal Status of Afghan Refugees in Pakistan, a Story of Eight Agreements and Two Suppressed Premises." *International Journal of Refugee Law* 20(2): 253–72.

Zolberg, A., A. Suhrke, and S. Aguayo. 1989. *Escape from Violence: Conflict and the Refugee Crisis in the Developing World*. Oxford: Oxford University Press.

Interviews with representatives of epistemic communities

Bo Nai, President, Chin Refugee Committee, Delhi. September 29, 2012

Dares Chusri, Country Director in Thailand, US Committee for Refugees and Immigrants. October 7, 2008.

Duniya Aslam Khan, Assistant Public Relations Officer, UNHCR Islamabad. October 9, 2012.

Gerald Martone, International Rescue Committee. May 16, 2008.

Jack Dunford, Director, Thai Burma Border Consortium. October 5, 2008.

Karten Tsering, President, New Aruna Nagar Colony, Resident Welfare Association. October 12, 2012.

Kitty McKinsey, Public Relations Officer, Headquarters of UN High Commissioner for Refugees for South-East Asia, Bangkok. October 16, 2008.

Lobsang Dorji, General Secretary, Regional Tibetan Youth Congress, Samyeling, Delhi. October 12, 2012.

Meghna Guhathakurta, Executive Director, Research Initiatives Bangladesh, Dhaka. October 15, 2012.

Moe Zaw Myint and Winmit Yosalawin at the BBC Burmese Service, Bangkok. October 20, 2008.

Supang Chantavanich and Premjai Vungsiriphaisal at Chulalongkorn University in Bangkok. October 27, 2008.

Thomas Albrecht, UN High Commissioner for Refugees, Washington, DC. May 16, 2008.

Timothy Scherer at the US Embassy in Thailand. October 17, 2008.

Yongyuth Chalamwong, Warowan Chadoevwit, and Kwanjai Lekagul at the Thai Development Research Institute. October 3, 2008.

Chronology of Events Relating to Refugee Creation, 1947–2012

Index

Page numbers in bold indicate text that appears within tables. Page numbers in italics indicate text within figures. An "n" next to a page number indicates that the text can be found in an endnote.

For Product Safety Concerns and Information please contact our EU
representative GPSR@taylorandfrancis.com
Taylor & Francis Verlag GmbH, Kaufingerstraße 24, 80331 München, Germany

www.ingramcontent.com/pod-product-compliance
Lightning Source LLC
Chambersburg PA
CBHW050518280326
41932CB00014B/2366

9 781138 948464